TWINS ON TWINS

TWINS ON TWINS

by Kathryn McLaughlin Abbe & Frances McLaughlin Gill

TEXT BY JULIE SZEKELY

RESEARCH BY VICTORIA B. BJORKLUND, Ph.D.

Clarkson N. Potter, Inc./Publishers

DISTRIBUTED BY CROWN PUBLISHERS, INC.

NEW YORK

Published by Clarkson N. Potter, Inc., One Park Avenue, New York, New York 10016 and simultaneously in Canada by General Publishing Company Limited

Manufactured in the United States of America

Library of Congress Cataloging in Publication Data
  Abbe, Kathryn McLaughlin.
    Twins on twins.

    Bibliography: p.
    Includes index.
    1. Twins.   I. Gill, Frances McLaughlin, joint author.   II. Title
    HQ784.T9G54   155.4′44   80-16156

ISBN: 0-517-55761-4 (pbk.)

10 9 8 7 6 5 4 3 2 1

First Paperback Edition, 1985

PHOTO CREDITS

ABC Television; page 82
Better Homes and Gardens © 1973; Meredith Corporation; page 174 top right
Bettmann Archive, Inc.; pages 20, 152 bottom
Michael Borum; pages 184–185
Brown Brothers; page 70
Bruckmann, Munich; page 28
Tilly Abbe Feldman; page 175, lower
Forum Gallery, NYC; page 52
Leslie Gill; page 13
Gareth Goodger-Hill; page 163
Good Housekeeping Magazine © 1970 The Hearst Corporation; page 174 top left
Midtown Gallery; pages 50–51
New York Public Library; pages 13, 18, 19, 64, 73
Lisa Fonssagrives Penn; page 171 bottom right
Kit Pinto-Coelho; page 167
Jane Smiley; page 68
The Conde Nast Publications, Inc.; courtesy *Glamour*, Jan. 1965 © 1964, page 174 bottom left and courtesy *Vogue*, Feb. 1, 1958 © 1958; page 172
William Wrigley, Jr., Company; page 57

Title page:
Rear; Linda Eisenberg and Larry Deverett
Front; Jeffrey Deverett and Leora Eisenberg

To James Abbe and Leslie Gill
for their boundless enthusiasm
and encouragement

ACKNOWLEDGMENTS

As we close *Twins on Twins* we remember with pleasure this last year, recalling those who contributed time and effort and suggestions. As the book grew we acquired a network of new friends and new sources. The response of museums, galleries and private art collectors everywhere was overwhelming. Our first thanks go to all who gave permission to reproduce their twin works of art. We acknowledge the kindness of Mrs. Ludlow Bull and Mrs. Merrell Stout for permission to publish their twin paintings and likewise of Mrs. John Davis and Mrs. Bouvier Putnam for welcoming us so graciously. Special thanks to Jane Smiley of the Mohonk Mountain House for her material on the Smiley twins and to Jolie Kelter and Michael Malce, to Kate and Joel Kopp, and Ann Phillips, our appreciation for their search for twin items and for their special finds, particularly of early photographs and objects.

Paula Pumplin of the Frick Art Reference Library helped locate the lovely Cuyp painting of the twin babies. Our thanks, also, to Alice Weaver, librarian of the rare books room at the New York Academy of Medicine, and to Margaret Mairs of the Stowe-Day Foundation for material on the Stowe family. The Schlesinger Library at Radcliffe College loaned letters by Harriet Beecher Stowe. We thank Mary Black of the New York Historical Society for her knowledgeable answers to our questions. Anthropologists Jane Safer and Laila Williamson provided material, suggestions and encouragement all along the way. We are grateful to Koren and Tom Abbe for their thoughts on the mythology and astrological aspect of twins and to John Barrett who gave careful thought to many of the twin themes in our book. We thank Marie Jeanne Adams of the Department of Anthropology at Harvard University and Professor Thomas Bouchard of the University of Minnesota's Twin Study project for their help and information.

Important material for the chapter "On Being Twins" came from many expert sources. Dr. Robert F. Thompson of Yale University very kindly loaned material on the Yoruba. We wish to thank Dr. Gordon Allen, a statistician at the National Institute of Mental Health, for his contribution, Dr. H. Warner Kloepfer of Tulane University for his information on twins' handprints and footprints and Dr. Blair O. Rogers for his vital information on skin grafting and transplants in relation to twins. Donald Keith and Dr. Louis Keith have been enormously helpful with thoughts on many aspects of twinship.

Our special thanks and gratitude go to Kathryn's husband, James, for sources of inspiration all during the work on the book, and to Frances's daughter, Leslie, for her skillful work on the presentation. James Seno, our photographic technician, and Danice English, research assistant, were tireless in helping with all details.

Our West Coast friends Margaretta and Frederick Mitchell offered hospitality and twin ideas during our visits with them. Eli Abbe and Jessica Arner of Palo Alto searched for twin subjects as did Tilly Feldman, who found our wonderful San Francisco twins, the Browns and the Jangs. Thanks, too, to Bob Cato and Si Litvinoff for locating twins in the Los Angeles area. Carol Cutler found our twins in Washington, D.C. Mrs. David Mahre helped us to keep in touch with her busy skier sons, Phil and Steven. We thank Lucinda and Robert Wallace for finding the Pennsylvania farmers, and for their kindness during our stay with them. We appreciate the cordial welcome extended to us by Beth Corley and Bebe Simmons at the convention of the International Twins Association last September.

We have had the rare good fortune of working with a truly creative editor, Carol Southern; we thank her for her loving attention and enthusiasm for *Twins on Twins* from the beginning. To Hermann Strohbach, our thanks for the book design. Dr. Victoria Bjorklund did special research, spending endless time with us during every phase of work on the book. To Julie Szekely very warm thanks for her skillful writing of the text and for the sensitivity and understanding she brought to the complex twin themes in *Twins on Twins*.

New York City, April 1980

CONTENTS

INTRODUCTION

We are twins. Our book is an exploration of being twins. As professional photographers since 1941, we have met many twins—as subjects of photo stories, as co-workers, as friends. As we read and thought about life as twins, we discovered intriguing patterns we wanted to pursue.

Twins on Twins is our first joint effort. Our book shows twins throughout history as they have been recorded in myth, painting and photography. Traditionally, twins in literature have been used to portray opposites: good vs. evil, light vs. dark, mortal vs. immortal. The relationship of the twins was used to create intrigue, express an antithesis or explore two aspects of a single personality. Most books about twins treat them as subjects of medical studies. People often think that these studies reflect the reality of being twins. We question that assumption, feeling that twins, as very similar yet very different people, have had little chance to speak for themselves. Our book is a first step in the telling of that story.

As photographers, our main interest has been to portray twins of today. Because the material on fraternals and multiples is so vast, that intriguing subject must remain for another book. For the section "Twins Now," we interviewed and photographed twenty-nine sets of look-alike and same-sex twins. For the other chapters we spoke with hundreds more. All the twins who agreed to talk with us responded with warmth and enthusiasm and, often, surprise, when asked how it felt to be a twin. Most enjoyed being twins. They were supportive of each other's projects and in some cases worked side by side in the same careers. They treated their relationship with patience and good humor. Many of them also pointed to a special need for privacy and recognition as individuals. We also spoke with parents, siblings and friends of twins. *Twins on Twins* presents the thoughts of hundreds of people, both twins and those who know and care about them.

We saw twins all over the United States, from Vermont to California, ranging in age from two weeks to one hundred years old. Some twins we met by chance, such, as the Janickis from Poland, who were visiting New York. We learned of others from newspaper articles or television programs and from asking everyone we met, "Do you know any twins?"

Discovering twins was one task. Catching up with them was quite another. Consider the problem of making an appointment with tennis players Tim and Tom Gullikson in the midst of sweltering heat and the tense competition for the U.S. Open Tennis Championship. For three days we tried to reach them, doubting they could speak to us immediately before a match. When we finally photographed them during a moment of rest in one of Manhattan's pocket parks, they gave us so much of their time that their wives came to urge them to leave for a crucial game.

When facing the busy schedule of interviewing and photographing our twins, our first thought was to divide the work. However, we soon found that twins did not relate to one of us in the same way they did to both. Talking with both of us encouraged a deeper sharing of feelings and experiences.

With some sets of twins we had unlimited time, and we each made our own interpretation. When we had only ten or fifteen minutes available, one of us would photograph and the other would ask questions. In certain circumstances, such as having but a few seconds during a circus performance, we photographed side by side. Because of the unity of our work, we have chosen to share the credit for all of the photographs.

The most moving part of our experience has been the pleasure of getting to know other twins so well. Each set of twins became special to us and became part of our lives. Not only are we grateful to them, but we appreciate all the cooperation given to us by their families and friends. These twins have become unforgettable to us. We hope they will become unforgettable to you.

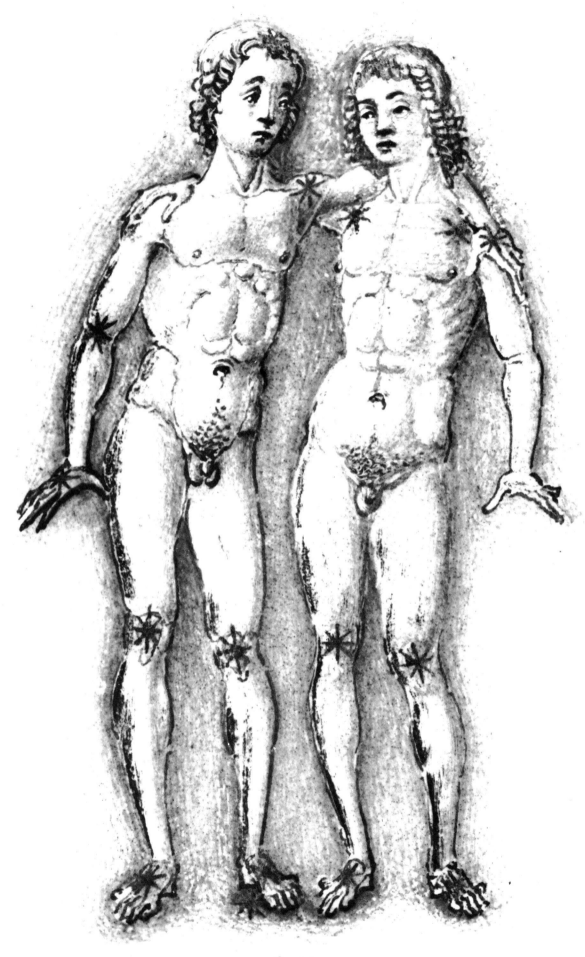

Gemini.
C. J. Hyginus, from Sideribus Tractatus Italy, Padua, c. 1450.
Spencer Collection, New York Public Libary.

TWINS IN MYTHOLOGY

Imagine, if you will, a primitive mind attempting to understand the birth of two children where one had been expected. In the absence of scientific description, it is no wonder that such an event might take on supernatural overtones. A twin birth during a successful harvest might have been considered a good omen, a visit from the gods. If, however, the birth coincided with drought, flood, famine or fire, it isn't difficult to imagine the twins being blamed for the disaster and being considered a portent of trouble.

People throughout the ages have both welcomed twins and feared them. The belief that twins were the possessors of supernatural powers can be traced back to earliest times. Twins sometimes were thought to be bearers of good fortune or to have second sight. In many of the folk tales the twins appear as gifted heroes, as magicians, as healing gods with miraculous powers such as the ability to forecast the weather, or control it, and the ability to promote or inhibit fertility. Sometimes, in these myths, one twin may be good and the other evil. One may symbolize darkness, the other light. One may represent the sun, while the other twin is the moon.

Among native American Indian tribes, there are many instances of twin legends. The Huron and Iroquois Indians have a similar story about the twins who they believe founded their tribes. The Huron tale describes Ataentsic, the moon goddess, who fell out of heaven into the primeval waters. Her virgin daughter gave birth to earth's first children, the twins Ioskeha (the White One) and Tawiscara (the Dark One), but died when the Dark One, refusing to be born in the usual manner, burst forth from his mother's armpit. Later the twins quarreled and Ioskeha killed his evil brother with a staghorn. Ioskeha then bestowed many gifts on mankind before returning to the sky as the Sun.

The twin hero legend appears in cultures and religions in every part of the world. Consider these twin tales through time:

Sicilian Mother Goddess with Twin Babies.
Collection of the Archaeological Museum, Syracuse, Italy.

Throughout history mankind has worshipped a mother goddess as the giver of
life. We call her Mother Earth and credit her for the fertility of fields and streams
and mankind itself. Many cultures depict her as a virgin and as the first mother of
twins. This sculpture of the Sicilian mother goddess, Hybaela with her twins, dates
from 600 B.C.

This 400 B.C. ruin of the Sanctuary of the Twin Gods in Agrigento, Sicily, shows that Castor and Pollux were worshipped in lands far from Greece. Mythology reports that after the conquest of the Golden Fleece, Castor and Pollux landed with the Argonauts in Sicily, where Jason honored the twin gods at a feast, "The Theoxenius," establishing the brothers as divinities in this area.

Aztec Mother Goddess, Xochiquetzal, and Her Twin Sons.
Kingsborough Manuscript, Codex Laud.

The mother goddess, Xochiquetzal, credited by the Aztecs with being the first mother of twins, is shown with her sons at her feet.

THE BOYS WITH THE GOLDEN STARS

In *The Violet Fairy Book* of 1901, Andrew Lang relates a tale of twins born of a young woman who had vowed to "give the man who chooses me two boys, twins, each with a golden star on his forehead, as bright as those in the sky."

A young emperor, overhearing the young woman's vow, took her at her word and whisked her away to his castle. Unfortunately, his stepmother had other ideas as to whom the emperor should wed, namely, her own daughter, and when the twins were born, she buried them outside the palace. Two aspen trees sprouted where they were buried and grew as no aspens ever had. "In each day they added a year's growth, and each night they added a year's growth, and at dawn, when the stars faded out of the sky, they grew three years' growth in the twinkling of an eye." The stepmother's daughter, who became empress after her mother buried the twins, and who knew of the trees' origin, begged the emperor to cut them down. After much coaxing, he agreed, but on the condition that one be used to make a bed for him, and the other a bed for the empress.

The next night, as the empress lay on her new bed, she heard it say, "Is it too heavy for you, little brother?" "Oh, no," she heard her husband's bed respond, "it is not heavy at all. I feel nothing but joy now that my beloved father rests over me." "It is very heavy for me," said the empress's bed, "for on me lies an evil soul."

Next morning, the empress made a huge fire of the beds. From the fire, two sparks escaped and, after floating through the air, fell into the river where they became two fish with golden scales. Later, when the emperor's fishermen caught the golden fish, they decided to take them to their master as a gift. "Do not take us there," said the fish, "for that is whence we came, and yonder lies our destruction." The fish directed the men instead to collect all the dew from the leaves and to let them swim in it; then to lay them in the sun until its rays had dried the dew. And when the sun had dried the dew, the fishermen found two young boys with hair as golden as the stars on their foreheads. The boys grew quickly. "In every day they grew a year's growth, and in every night another year's growth, but at dawn, when the stars were fading, they grew three years' growth in the twinkling of an eye. And they grew in other things besides height. Thrice in age, and thrice in wisdom, and thrice in knowledge."

"Now take us to our father," they said, and the fishermen, giving each a lambskin hat to cover their stars, did so.

"Who are you?" asked the emperor.

"We are twins," said the boys, "two shoots from one stem, which has been broken, and half lies in the ground and half sits at the head of this table. We have traveled a long way; we have spoken in the rustle of the wind, have whispered in the wood, we have sung in the waters, but now we wish to tell you a story which you know without knowing it, in the speech of men."

After telling their tale they lifted their caps, and their golden hair and golden stars were revealed. Thereafter, their mother sat next to her husband at the head of the table, the stepmother's daughter became a sewing maid, the stepmother was tied to a wild horse to wander forever, and everyone knew and has never forgotten that whoever has a mind turned to wickedness is sure to come to a very bad end.

CASTOR & POLLUX, OU LES GEMEAUX.

Castor and Pollux, or the Twins.

Castor und Pollux, oder die Zwillinge.

Castor en Pollux, of de Tweelingen.

CASTOR & POLLUX

Zeus, chief among ancient Greek mythological gods and ruler of the heavens, was fond of pursuing women under the guise of various benign creatures. One day while Leda, the wife of Sparta's King Tyndareus, was bathing in a river frequented by swans, Zeus appeared as a swan and threw himself into her arms. Though she was already with child, Zeus' embrace was not unfruitful. Leda is said to have delivered two eggs. One produced Castor and Clytemnestra, the children of her husband. The other produced Pollux and Helen, whose father was Zeus. Though children of different fathers, Castor and Pollux were identical, and their devotion set a pattern of brotherly love. Their deeds were so worthy that they were considered divine not only in Sparta and other parts of Greece, but also in Sicily and Italy.

The eighteenth-century author B. Picart Le Romain wrote of them:

The two brothers, Castor and Pollux, having scoured the Aegean Sea of the pirates that infested it, the Greeks worshipped them as the tutelar gods of navigation. What contributed not a little to their having divine honors paid them, was an adventure they had in their voyage to Colchis. The Argonauts were in great danger of perishing in a violent storm. Orpheus made a vow to the gods of the sea and immediately two flames of fire were seen to light on the heads of Castor and Pollux and the storm ceased. From that time, those fires had the name of Castor and Pollux; and their appearing in a storm was looked upon as a happy omen of fair weather. If there appeared but one it was a sinister presage; because those two brothers having always lived in the strictest friendship, their separation was thought to portend nothing but destruction.

Known as Saint Elmo's fire, this phenomenon today is called a corposant, from the Latin *corpus sanctum*, meaning "holy body," and defined as a light, due to atmospheric electricity, sometimes seen on the mastheads and yardarms of ships, and on church towers and treetops.

APOLLO: "Can't you tell me how to distinguish Castor and Pollux, for they are so alike that I'm constantly out."

HERMES: "He that was with us yesterday is Castor."

APOLLO: "How can you possibly distinguish between two persons so like one another?"

HERMES: "Pollux's face is all black and blue with the blows he received in wrestling, and particularly from Bebryx, in the expedition of the Argonauts."

APOLLO: "I am very much obliged to you for letting me know this distinguishing mark, for I always confounded them, each having alike his egg-shell, helmet, his white horse, his javelin and his star. But I say, why do we never see Castor and Pollux at the same time?"

HERMES: "Well, they are so fond of each other that when fate decreed one of them must die and only one be immortal, they decided to share immortality between them."

APOLLO: "Not wise, Hermes. What proper employment can they engage in, that way? I foretell the future; Aesculapius cures diseases; you are a good messenger—but these two, are they to idle away their whole time?"

HERMES: "No surely. They're in Poseidon's service. Their business is to save any ship in distress."

APOLLO: "Ah, now you say something. I'm delighted they're in such a good business."

—Lucian A.D. 120–180

Castor and Pollux, or the Twins.
Designed and engraved by Bernard Picart from *The Temple of Muses*, 1733. Prints Division, New York Public Library.

Castor and Pollux.
Image from Greek vase. Fourth century, B.C.

The 400 B.C. vase was found in 1865 during excavation of the necropolis of Kameiros in Rhodes. We see Castor and Pollux, naked under their red capes, hovering over a bed that has been prepared for their arrival at a feast in their honor. Believing that the gods rewarded those who spread before them hospitable tables, the Greeks had a yearly celebration for Castor and Pollux called "The Theoxenius." Since Castor and Pollux were considered the gods of hospitality, a feast in their honor was a public event, even strangers knew they would be welcome. To spare Castor and Pollux the boredom of only mortal company, an invitation in their name was made to Helen and Hercules. The Athenian meal offered every year consisted of cheese, barley, leeks, and ripe olives. During the feast the gods reclined on their bed, which here is shown with two mattresses. Notice that the gods arrive from the left, which was always a good omen.

The brothers were called Dioscuri, sons of Jupiter, and as protectors of mariners, they were honored in temples built along dangerous routes, such as the Bosporus Strait and the North Sea. Ancient mariners frequently called their ships by the names *Castor* and *Pollux*, thus hoping to win a safe passage. In the Book of Acts, St. Luke, speaking of St. Paul's voyage to Rome, says, "After three months, we set sail in a ship of Alexandria, whose name was Castor and Pollux and with the Twin Brothers as figurehead." After their return from the Argonauts' adventure, they rescued their sister Helen from Theseus, who had carried her off to Attica. The brothers invaded and took the town, defeating the Athenians who were assisting Theseus, and rescued their sister.

It was believed that by their mere appearance on the battlefield, on their beautiful white horses, victory was assured for whichever side they chose. Their most famous apparition was to aid the Romans against the Latins in the battle of Lake Regillus, around 496 B.C. The Greek historian Dionysius Halicarnassus described that event:

It is said that in this battle, two men on horseback, far excelling in both beauty and stature those our human stock produces, and just growing their first beard, appeared to Postumius, the dictator, and to those arrayed about him, and charged at the head of the Roman horse, striking with their spears all the Latins they encountered and driving them headlong before them.[1]

Later, Castor and Pollux fell in love with their uncle's daughters Phoebe and Hilaira, who were already betrothed to Idas and Lynceus. During a fight, Pollux slew Lynceus and Castor was killed by Idas. Grieved, Pollux begged to share his brother's fate. Zeus, to comfort his son, allowed him to share his immortality with Castor. He placed them in the sky, where they form the constellation Gemini. One star of Gemini rises as the other sets—Castor and Pollux taking turns living one day on earth and the next among the gods of Olympus. People born during late May through late June, when the constellation dominates the sky, are said to have dual characteristics.

Coin of Castor and Pollux.
c. 200 B.C. A coin from the Brutti (Italians), who from 280 to 150 B.C. conquered most of the Hellenic states of southern Italy. On one side are the heads of Castor and Pollux and on the other, their whole figures on horseback. Note the stars above their heads on both sides. The coin was probably copied from a Greek coin and authorized for use by the Romans.

Faustulus Brings the
Twins Romulus and Remus
to Acca Larentia.
Alexander Anderson after Edward
Francis Burney, c. 1700.
Engraving, British.
Stauffer Collection,
New York Public Library.

Romulus and Remus
Being Suckled by the Wolf
or *The She-Wolf.*
Capitoline Museum, Rome.

ROMULUS & REMUS

It is said the ruler Proca had two sons. To the elder, Numitor, he gave rule of the Silvian family. His brother Amulius, however, drove Numitor out and assumed the role, killing Numitor's son. He appointed Numitor's daughter, Rhea, to be among the virgins guarding the sacred and perpetual fire of Vesta, goddess of the hearth. As a vestal virgin she was consigned to perpetual chastity; thus he deprived her of the chance to have children. However, Rhea gave birth to twin sons and named Mars, the god of war, as father of the children. Amulius had Rhea manacled and thrown into prison and ordered that the infants be drowned in the Tiber. The men assigned this gruesome task, however, left the twins in a basket floating on a stagnant pool off the regular channel of the river. When the water receded, the basket was left high and dry. There, the children were found by a wolf who heard their cries when she came to drink. As she was nursing and cleaning them, the keeper of the royal flock, Faustulus, found them and took them to his hut for his wife, Acca Larentia, to rear.

As the boys grew, they became so strong that they faced wild beasts in the mountains and would attack robbers, dividing the robbers' spoils among their fellow shepherds. Thus their group of comrades grew.

One year, while participating in a celebration, Romulus and Remus were recognized and ambushed by robbers they had previously attacked. Romulus defended himself successfully, but Remus was captured and taken to King Amulius. Charged with having raided the land of Numitor, he was turned over to the dethroned king for punishment. Numitor, however, was intrigued by Remus' age and twin status, both of which reminded him of his grandsons. And Faustulus, who from the very beginning had suspected the twins' true identity, chose this time to reveal the facts to Romulus. Romulus called on his fellow shepherds to launch a surprise attack on the king, and Remus came with men from Numitor's land to help his brother. Romulus killed Amulius and gave credit to his grandfather Numitor for the victory. The brothers hailed their grandfather as king and the town confirmed the title.

Having accomplished this feat, Romulus and Remus decided to found their own city in the same place in which they had been left to die. Since they did not know who had been born first, they decided to look for an omen from the gods to determine who should give the new city its name and who should govern it. They separated to two hills. Remus is said to have been the first to receive an omen, in the form of a flight of six vultures. This was already reported when Romulus said he had seen *twelve* vultures. Each claimed priority: Remus by seeing the birds first and Romulus by seeing more of them. The two quarreled and Remus mockingly leaped over a wall begun by Romulus. In rage, Romulus plunged his sword into Remus, saying, "So perish whoever else shall leap over my walls!" Thus Romulus acquired sole power, and the city, founded in 753 B.C., was called Rome. Thus was born the practice of killing any soldier who scaled the city's walls.

ESAU & JACOB

From the Book of Genesis we learn of the fraternal twins Esau and Jacob. Isaac, the son of Abraham, was forty years old when he married Rebekah, and he entreated God because Rebekah was barren. Rebekah conceived and when she had been pregnant seven months, she began to wish that the curse of childlessness had not been removed from her. She suffered torturous pain because her twin sons began their lifelong quarrels in her womb. Rebekah asked for an explanation. "And the Lord said unto her, Two nations are in thy womb, and two manner of people shall be separated from thy bowels; and the one people shall be stronger than the other people; and the elder shall serve the younger." At the time of birth, the first, Esau, came out red all over like a hairy garment. As he was being delivered, his brother reached out and grabbed his heel, and then Jacob emerged smooth and white. Esau grew to be a hunter and was favored by his father, "because he did eat of his venison." But Rebekah preferred Jacob.

One day when Jacob had prepared a pot of lentil soup, Esau came in from the field faint with hunger and begged to be fed. Jacob said, "Sell me this day thy birthright." Esau, feeling that he was on the point of death and that his birthright was worthless, sold it to Jacob for soup and bread.

Years later, when Isaac was so old he could hardly see, he told Esau to go to the field and return with venison so that he might eat some of it before blessing him. Rebekah overheard her husband and told Jacob to fetch two young goats to be prepared and taken to his father so that Jacob might receive the blessing. Jacob replied, "Behold Esau my brother is a hairy man and I am a smooth man." Rebekah told him to obey her and he did. Then Rebekah dressed Jacob in Esau's clothes and covered his hands and neck with the skins of the goats. When Jacob presented himself to his father, Isaac may have suspected the hoax, for he told Jacob to come closer "that I may feel thee, my son, whether thou be my very son Esau or not." When he felt Jacob's goatskin-covered hands, he said, "The voice is Jacob's voice, but the hands are the hands of Esau." So Jacob received the blessing due the firstborn.

When Esau returned with the venison, his father realized he'd been tricked and said, "Thy brother came and hath taken away thy blessing."

As the result of this deceit Esau hated Jacob; his plans to kill him were thwarted only by Rebekah's timely intervention. Twenty years later Esau met his guilty brother and received him without malice.

COSMAS & DAMIAN

The most celebrated patrons of medicine and pharmacy in all Christian countries are the twins Cosmas and Damian. Cosmas, the physician, and Damian, the apothecary, were known not only for their medical successes, but also for their devout Christian faith. They lived at the Turkish seaport of Argae in Cilicia and traveled from place to place to heal the sick, taking every opportunity to spread the zeal they felt for their faith. Because they accepted no payment for their services, they were called *Anargyroi*, meaning "Silverless." Possibly because they accepted no fee, they were successful in converting many to Christianity.

In the year A.D. 292, when religious persecution under the Roman Emperor Diocletian was raging, Cosmas and Damian happened to visit the city of Lycia, where the anti-Christian Governor Lysias of Cilicia apprehended and attempted to kill them. He threw them first into the sea, then into a furnace and, when these efforts failed, he tried to crucify them. While they were hanging on the crosses, a mob tried to stone them, but the stones recoiled to their own heads. In addition, the arrows of archers ordered to shoot at Cosmas and Damian boomeranged in the air and returned, scattering the bowmen. Finally, in 303, Lysias had the twins beheaded. Their bodies were carried into Syria, and buried at Cyrrhus, the chief center of their cult, but even their death did not stop their work. Many miracles of healing were said to have occurred at their hand after their death. Sometimes they would appear to sufferers in their sleep, prescribing treatment or immediately curing them. Among those who attributed recovery from serious illness to Cosmas and Damian was the Byzantine Emperor Justinian I, who honored the city of Cyrrhus and built two churches at Constantinople in honor of the twins.

J. Rendel Harris in his 1906 book, *The Cult of the Heavenly Twins*, made a case for Cosmas and Damian's having "displaced" Castor and Pollux, re-

Cosmas and Damian.
G. B. Carraciola. The Prado Museum,
Madrid.

manifesting eight hundred years later. Harris describes a raft trip in 1903 down the Euphrates River during which, just before entering a canyon marked by a series of treacherous rapids, he noticed a ruined building on a cliff. Asking what castle it was, he was told, "It is no castle, it is the ruined church of Saint Cosmas and Saint Damian." "It was evident," Harris said, "that there had been a shrine of the saints towards which men prayed before shooting the rapids. We thus discover," he continues, "not only that Cosmas and Damian were at home on the upper Euphrates, but that they were discharging there, what one would not at first have expected, the function of protecting those who travel by water, which is one of the chief duties of the Twin Brethren."

TWINS IN ART

What a challenge to paint twins! The artist does not simply paint one person twice. Rather, he must record each of the twins as individuals; must be aware of subtle differences between the two in such things as hand gesture, tilt of the head, and the look in the eye, whether a direct gaze or a downward or sideward glance. The true artist notices these differences quickly, and delights in his sensitive observations.

Through the centuries families traditionally commissioned formal portraits of themselves and their children, and in some cases these children were twins. In the pages that follow are paintings of twins made by artists from many countries, many backgrounds, through many eras. Some of the painters were so skilled and highly trained that one could guess their work had been commissioned by royal families and monied patrons; others were itinerant painters who worked in a simpler tradition. All the twin paintings share one outstanding quality: the twins appear to have been treasured by their families. Artists, such as Waldo Peirce and Elmer MacRae, exulted in making paintings of their own twins. In the painting of the Cobham family, the twins occupy a favored spot in the center of the group.

The painting that appears on the opposite page is part of Kathryn and James Abbe's collection of twins in art. About twenty years ago the Abbes spotted an art dealer walking down a Manhattan street with this work under his arm. They followed him to his gallery and made their first "twin" purchase. Their twin collection now includes daguerreotypes and early photographs, prints, watercolors, books and everyday objects from doorstops to pillowcases. "Nothing is too small or too odd to consider," says Kathryn, "but the image must say 'twins.'"

Twin Boys.
A. J. Pawling, American, c. 1830, oil on canvas. Collection of James and Kathryn Abbe.

The Cholmondeley Sisters.
Artist unknown, c. 1610, oil on panel.
Tate Gallery, London.

Though they seemed identical, these women, portrayed as *Two Ladies of the Cholmondeley Family*, were painted with different colored eyes. The woman and child on the left have blue eyes, while the woman and child on the right have brown. This difference indicates that they must have been fraternal twins, though the inscription on the painting leaves even their twinship in doubt:

> Two ladies of the Cholmondeley Family
> Who were born on the same day,
> Married the same day,
> And brought to bed the same day.

Perhaps they were the daughters or nieces of Lady Mary and Sir Hugh Cholmondeley. Perhaps they married into the Cholmondeley family and coincidentally had a striking resemblance to each other. Art historians credit the Dutch artist Marcus Gheeraerts with having made the portrait around 1610. It hangs in the Tate Gallery in London.

The Cobham Family.
Hans Eworth, British, seventeenth century,
oil on canvas. Courtauld Collection Library.

The Twins.
Jacob von Gerritsz Cuyp, Dutch School,
early seventeenth century,
oil on canvas. Location unknown.

The Twins.
Cornelius de Vos, Dutch School, c. 1630,
oil on canvas. Ateneum Museum, Helsinki.
Sinebrychoff Collection.

Triptych with Romulus and Remus.
Detail, artist unknown, German,
sixteenth century. Nuremberg National
Museum, Germany.

Triptych with Romulus and Remus.
Right panel, artist unknown, German,
sixteenth century. Nuremberg National
Museum, Germany.

Faustulus Bringing the Twins Romulus and Remus to Acca Larentia.
Artist unknown, Flemish School, c. seventeenth century.

The De Peyster Twins.
Artist unknown, American, c. 1728, oil on canvas.
Abby Aldrich Rockefeller Folk Art Center, Williamsburg, Virginia.

The painting on the opposite page shows Eve and Catherine De Peyster who were twin daughters of Margareta Van Cortlandt De Peyster and Abraham De Peyster, once treasurer of New York Province. Eve died at the age of four, shortly after this painting was made in 1728. Catherine married John Livingston, grandson of the first Lord of the Manor of Livingston. She lived until 1804. The portrait is a fine example of the work of America's first school of artists, the Patroon Painters who were active in the Hudson River Valley in the early eighteenth century. The wreath, floor, and balustrade details point to Dutch tradition, while the direct gaze and bare feet of the girls were unique to paintings of the New World.

John W. Clark and Henry L. Clark.
William Jennys, American, c. 1800, oil on canvas.
Collection of Mrs. Ludlow Bull.

Joseph and Sigmund Paul DeGhéquière.
F. Barrois, American. c. 1810, drawing on paper.
Collection of Mrs. Merrell F. Stout.

Twin Sisters.
Artist unknown, American, c. 1840, oil on canvas.
Collection of Edgar William and Bernice Chrysler Garbisch.

The Twin Sisters.
Artist unknown, American, c. 1835, oil on canvas.
Collection of James and Kathryn Abbe.

The Twin Sisters.
Artist unknown, American, c. 1840.
Mystic Seaport Museum, Mystic, Connecticut.

Figureheads, thought to bring luck to mariners,
traditionally were placed at the bows of ships to lead
them safely through the seas. This sculpture, carved in
1840, is the only known figurehead of identical twins.
Their twinship brings to mind Castor and Pollux, the
twin brothers who were patron saints of ancient
seafarers.

The Ten Broeck Twins.
Ammi Phillips, American, c. 1834, oil on canvas.
Private Collection.

Jacob and William Ten Broeck and Their Wives, Sara Ann and Mary Jane.
Ira Chaffee Goodell, American, c. 1880, charcoal drawing over photograph.
Collection of Roderic H. Blackburn.

Ammi Phillips has been described as "the best, the most prolific, and the most inventive American country portrait painter of the nineteenth century," and a "nearly perfect example of the self-taught painter who experimented to find solutions to his own painting problems." Phillips was born in 1788 in Colebrook, Connecticut, in the foothills of the Berkshires. At the age of twenty-five, he took his bride to Rensselaer County, New York, later moving his family down to Rhinebeck. Through his portrait painting, Phillips not only supported a family and purchased property, but also recorded the complicated interrelationship of the Livingston, Ten Broeck and Sanders families in Columbia County.

In 1834, Phillips took his canvas and paints to Hudson to make portraits of the sixth and seventh generations of the Ten Broeck family. Among those he painted were Jacob Wessel Ten Broeck, his wife, Anna Benner, and their eleven-year-old twin sons, Jacob Wessel and William Henry. The

boys were raised in Clermont on one of the largest fruit orchards in New York State at the time and are shown in their portrait with a still-life of peaches and pears. As the firstborn, Jacob inherited the family Bible and the family homestead in Germantown, while William was given the summer home in Hudson.

"In the early 1920s," says a Ten Broeck relative, "Uncle Evarts went out to visit at Jacob's house. The painting was on the junk pile to be pitched." Uncle Evarts Ten Broeck retrieved the portrait of the twins and that of their younger brother Andrew, also by Phillips. "That's how we got them."

The second twin, William, was married first, to Mary Jane Evarts. A year later, in 1848, Jacob was married to Mary Jane's twin sister, Sara Ann. Portraits of the two sets of twins were finely drawn in charcoal, possibly over photographs, by Ira Chaffee Goodell, in the 1880s. Born in 1800, Goodell, like Phillips, prepared portraits of locally prominent Columbia County residents.

The Siamese Twins, Chang and Eng.
Artist unknown, American, 1852, engraving after a daguerreotype.
Gleason's Pictorial Drawing Room Companion, March 1853.

SIAMESE TWINS

☞ For Day only.

THE
UNITED BROTHERS, CHANG-ENG,

This passage on the famous Siamese twins, Chang and Eng, is taken from *Gleason's Pictorial Drawing Room Companion*, March 19, 1853:

On the page herewith, we give a large and finely executed picture of Chang and Eng, the famous united Siamese twins, who were born in the city of Breklong(?) in Siam, in May 1811. They were brought to this country by the captain of the Ship Sachem (Coffin), arriving in August 1829.

They were at once brought before the public for exhibition, and during the twelve ensuing years, were visited by millions of people, taking in the course of their travels, the United States, Great-Britain, France, Holland and Belgium.

They are united to each other by a ligature, or band, about three and a half inches in length, and eight in circumference, formed at the extremity of the breast bone of each, extending downwards to the abdomen. . . .

Having secured a competence by exhibiting themselves, they settled in Wilkes County, North Carolina, but afterwards removed to Mt. Airy, Surry County, where they now reside.

Soon after taking up their abode in this region, they simultaneously became smitten with the charms of two very pretty sisters, named Yates, and each selecting his partner, the four were made two with all due ceremony. This double union has apparently proved highly satisfactory to all concerned.

The ladies are represented as amiable and interesting, while it is certain that the twins are devotedly attached to their wives.

At the present time Mr. Eng's six and Mr. Chang's five children, all of whom are apt scholars, are remarkably well behaved. They are also of a very prepossessing appearance, and are great favorites in their community.

The illustration will give a perfect idea of the appearance of the families, every likeness being copied from daguerreotypes, taken especially for the purpose.

In closing these remarks on the twins and their families, we would say that they seem to be remarkably happy, enjoy good health, have ample luxuries of life, and bid fair, as far as human judgment may go, to live many more years of domestic happiness and comfort. They are both naturalized citizens of our country.

The Twins.
D. W. Kellogg, American, 1845, lithograph.
Collection of James and Kathryn Abbe.

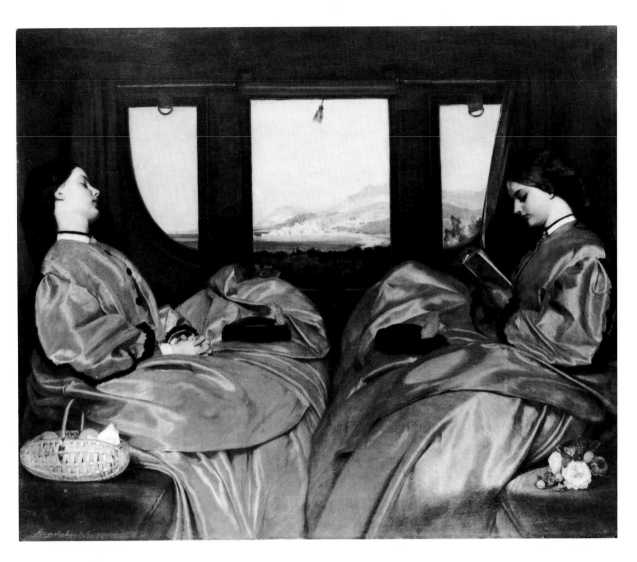

The Travelling Companions.
Augustus Egg, British, c. 1865, oil on canvas.
City of Birmingham Museum, England.

Kiss Me Quick.
Currier and Ives, American, 1835, lithograph.

"Children, this is the third time within the hour that I
have placed your hats properly upon your heads— there!"
Collection of Raynham Hall, Oyster Bay, New York.

Daughters by the Sea.
Elmer MacRae, American, c. 1910, oil on canvas.
Collection of Greenwich Historical Society,
Greenwich, Connecticut.

The Twins.
Elmer MacRae, American, c. 1910, oil on canvas.
Collection of Greenwich Historical Society,
Greenwich, Connecticut.

Under Gemini, published in 1966, provides personal glimpses into the treasured memories of one twin, Isabel Bolton, whose sister was swept out to sea at the age of fourteen in a sailing accident.

What a perfect summer day! It was exactly as we remembered it, confirmed by the vibrations of every nerve. There was the lightship, there were a trawler and a tugboat and a string of barges. There were no white caps today, it would be calm at the beaches. Would the tide be low or high when we got there? How could we wait for breakfast to be over? What should we wear when we went down? There were the blue cotton dresses, the brown dresses and the white ones. Which would Aunt Anna tell us we should not have put on? She'd rather have us wear the dark dresses and our heavy stockings and the high laced boots and our flannel pettycoats.

Completely at one decision, we got up and began to dress in our plainest and heaviest clothes. They would, we expected, be breakfasting on the pavillion. We must not be late, but we didn't want to be the first to arrive.

Dawdling, exchanging the emotions that were filling our heart, we arrayed ourselves in our least attractive costumes and descended to breakfast.

This excerpt from Isabel Bolton's *Under Gemini* seems to describe Elmer MacRae's painting *Daughters by the Sea*, which immortalized his twins Clarissa and Constant.

MacRae, born in New York City in 1875, was one of the group of artists who formed the Cos Cob School and organized the International Exhibition of Modern Art, which became renowned as the Armory Show of 1913. MacRae continued to work in varied media until his death in 1953.

Two Sisters.
Albert Herter, American, 1926, oil on canvas.
Private Collection.

The Bouvier Twins.
Alice Marsh, American, c. 1911,
painting on ivory.
Private Collection.

Maude and Michelle Bouvier (aunts to Jacqueline Bouvier Kennedy Onassis) were throughout their youth favorite subjects of photographers and painters, who vied for the privilege of reproducing their already duplicated beauty. The honor went to Albert Herter, whose portrait, *Two Sisters*, is considered one of his most successful studies. Herter was primarily a mural painter and tapestry designer but was enchanted by the twins' auburn hair and offered to paint them for nothing, provided he could exhibit the finished product on extended tour. "Remember, Michelle, how long we had to pose? I got tired of you leaning on my arm," Maude re-

called fifty-three years after their 1926 sitting. At the time, Michelle had just become engaged and wore a full-length peach taffeta gown with floral embroidery. Maude's pink chiffon dress was actually a short flapper style, but was portrayed as a long gown. The twins were surprise additions to the family of Maude Sargeant and John Vernou Bouvier, Jr. As children, they were photographed in profile by Arnold Genthe, and painter Alice Marsh reproduced their images on ivory. Having been told that Maude's skin was the color of cream and Michelle's the color of milk, Michelle always longed for skin the color of cream.

The Pipe Bearers.
Waldo Peirce, American, 1931,
oil on canvas.
Private Collection.

In 1949 a newspaper article called them "the most painted children in America." Michael Peirce and Mellen Chamberlin ("Bill") Peirce were born in Paris in 1930, where their father, Waldo Peirce, had been a student at Julien Academy, and where his work was regularly exhibited. Peirce, born in Bangor, Maine, educated at Harvard, recorded his twin children's activities with apparent relish. They are drawn at birth, when they were actually near death; then a week later, when they were stronger; then at age one month. They were drawn while nursing, learning to walk, running, eating, and even sitting on the potty. A Frick Museum reproduction of *The Pipe Bearers* has the notation: "A Peirce portrait of the Peirce twins, whose fun, according to Hemingway, 'is for one to hit Waldo over the head with a beer bottle while the other sets fire to his beard.'" Today the twins are photographers. Bill lives in London and Mike in Cambridge, Massachusetts.

Waldo Peirce is represented in the permanent collections of the Metropolitan Museum of Art, Whitney Museum, Brooklyn Museum, Butler Art Institute, Addison Gallery, Pennsylvania Academy and Farnsworth Museum.

Haircut by the Sea.
Waldo Peirce, American, 1934, oil on canvas.
Metropolitan Museum of Art.

Double Portrait (Self-Portrait with Moses Soyer).
Raphael Soyer, American, 1963, oil on canvas.
Private Collection.

Raphael Soyer in His Studio, 1979.

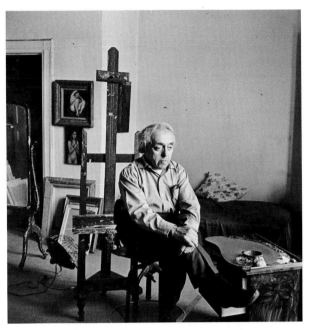

Moses Soyer in His Studio, 1972.

I painted both images from the mirror. I always paint from a model. It took several weeks for me to finish this painting. I painted Moses a lot. He's my twin brother and I liked to paint him, even later on when he became ill. The illness distorted his body, but even then he had a look on him that was magnificent. We were very close. His studio was not far from mine, on West Third Street. I was on East Third. We would call each other every day on the phone. We spoke Russian.

We looked exactly alike. People would greet me and say, "Hello, Moses," and Moses would be greeted with, "Hello Raphael." And I remember, a long time ago, I was walking along Fifth Avenue very briskly, and then I see Moses walking along too, and I was astounded. I mean, I didn't expect Moses to be there at that time. But it turned out to be myself, my reflection in the mirror, from far away.

We disliked being confused. There is kind of a desire to be oneself and it was a struggle. There was an awful lot of rivalry—sibling rivalry, I would call it—between the two of us. We tried to outdo one another. In childhood, our parents would say, "Moses did a better drawing than you." They didn't realize the effect this had—it was meant to be encouraging. Even in the school in Russia, the teacher would say, "You see, Moses is getting ahead of you."

Moses died just five years ago, in 1974. We were in London at that time and my daughter telephoned. "Don't come," she said, "it's too late." He died suddenly at work. He was painting a dancer, and he said to her, "Phyllis, don't cry." He was gone. He worked despite his illness. A very courageous man.

Raphael and Moses Soyer each are represented in the permanent collections of most major museums, including the Metropolitan Museum of Art, the Museum of Modern Art, the Whitney Museum, the Brooklyn Museum, the Phillips Collection, and the Hirshhorn Museum and Sculpture Garden.

The Twins.
William King, American, 1974, aluminum sculpture.

"Let's see, the arm came down and I put the little kid
at the end of it. And the other arm came down and was
resting on a chair, and I thought, 'I know what I'll do.
I'll put the same kid on the end of it.' To have the thing
stand up, you have to have three points to it, like a three-
legged stool. They are absolute mirror-image twins."

The Twins.
Paul Klee, 1946, charcoal drawing.
Private Collection.

"Won't you come home, Bill Bailey?"
Drawing for Christmas greeting card, c. 1900.
Collection of James and Kathryn Abbe.

"Won't you come home BILL BAILEY?
Won't you come home?
At such a time as this you shouldn't roam,
Of Christmas gifts for you,
There's waiting One or Two,
BILL BAILEY when you DO come Home."

The Original French Twin Sisters: Minnie and Lena.
Photographer unknown, c. 1890.
Billy Rose Collection, New York
Public Library at Lincoln Center.

TWINS IN PHOTOGRAPHY

Twins posed double problems as subjects for photographers in the mid-nineteenth century. When dealing with exposures of six seconds or longer, the photographer had to be inventive in his use of props to anchor fidgety hands and squirmy heads. Children who seem frozen or solemn in some of these early pictures might well have been warned not to move. Photographing twins afforded the photographer a rare opportunity to apply symmetry to composition, and tested his eye for such details as the tilt of a head or the level of shoulders. Above all, early photographers seem to have made twins look as identical as possible.

An early daguerreotype, complete with case, cost two dollars at a time when the average wage for a working man was two dollars a week. Still, lines formed outside studios, as portrait photography somewhat replaced portrait painting. It was a novelty to be photographed. While the painter colored his representations with personal impressions, the camera was impartial in its accurate imagery. People everywhere wanted to see what they really looked like. And many were interested in a permanent record of themselves for posterity, such as one woman of whom it was recorded, "As she planned a Western tour involving crossing the Alleghenies in winter, having heard about the risks of stagecoach travel, with horses at full downhill run over sheets of ice, she made out a will, 'had my daguerreotype taken for father,' and purchased her ticket."

Daguerreotype.
Photographer unknown, c. 1857.
Collection of James and Kathryn Abbe.

Daguerreotype.
Photographer unknown, c. 1854.
Collection of Joel and Kate Kopp.

Daguerreotype.
Photographer unknown, c. 1855.
Collection of James and Kathryn Abbe.

Ambrotype.
Photographer unknown, c. 1868.
Collection of James and Kathryn Abbe.

Harriet and Eliza Stowe.
Daguerreotype, photographer unknown. c. 1855.
Collection of the Schlesinger Library, Radcliffe College.

Nook Farm.
Home of the Stowe family
in Hartford, Connecticut.

This daguerreotype of Harriet Beecher Stowe's twins was probably made at about the time her book, *Uncle Tom's Cabin*, was published in 1852.

The twins were born on September 29, 1836, nine months after Harriet Beecher married Calvin Ellis Stowe, a theology professor. Following tradition, the couple had chosen the name of Stowe's deceased first wife, Eliza Tyler, for their first daughter. While away from home at the time of the birth, Stowe received word that his wife had borne twins and had named the second one Isabella. To this news, he responded:

Dear dear wife,
Bravo! you noble creature. The Lord be praised! Eliza and Harriet! Eliza and Harriet! Eliza and Harriet! Nothing short of that, my dear one. No names but these will ever pass my lips, I can assure you. Their names are Eliza and Harriet.

Four more children were born to Harriet Beecher Stowe, the last one three years prior to her completion of *Uncle Tom's Cabin*. The work's tremendous popularity not only enhanced the family's financial circumstances, but also jettisoned them into a new social life. Hattie and Eliza were now considered true young ladies and began to acquire fashionable clothes and to travel and study abroad, learning foreign languages, visiting art galleries and attending concerts. While Calvin Stowe voiced concern that his daughters' interests were becoming too material, his wife took pleasure in granting her daughters privileges which had been unavailable to her. Hattie and Eliza repaid her generosity with lifetime devotion.

Neither twin seems to have been interested in trading the companionship of the other for that of a husband. They are described as having been "perhaps unusually devoted to their mother and father," and "quite proud of their role as mother's lieutenants." Over the years, Hattie and Eliza became totally responsible for domestic decisions, in addition to serving as secretaries for both parents, taking dictation, answering correspondence, proofreading and serving as liaison with publishers.

When the twins were thirty-seven years old, the Stowes moved to the Hartford, Connecticut, neighborhood known as Nook Farm, where their home was a stone's throw from that of Samuel Clemens. Hattie and Eliza are said to have spent their days attending to household tasks in the morning, leaving their afternoons free for visiting. In an 1876 letter to George Eliot, Harriet Beecher Stowe wrote, "My twin daughters relieve me from all domestic care; they are lively, vivacious, with a real genius for practical life."

In 1884, their mother published her thirty-second and last book, *Our Famous Women*. Two years later, their father died, a death followed by that of their uncle and youngest sister.

Shortly after these tragedies, Mrs. Stowe's mind failed, and she became totally dependent on her twin daughters. When she died in 1896, Hattie and Eliza were by her side.

After their mother's death the twins moved to Simsbury, Connecticut, to be near their brother Charles, who was pastor of the Congregational Church. There they lived comfortably on the income left by their mother, enjoying the company of neighborhood children and looking after pet cats and birds. In 1907 Hattie died at the age of seventy-one, followed by the death of her sister five years later.

Twin Sisters: Iona and Viola Misick.
Charles D. Mosher, 1872, albumen print.
Photographic World, January 1873.

This excerpt about Iona and Viola Misick appeared in the December 1872 issue of *Photographic World.*

Not long since, we took occasion to speak of the difficulties attaching themselves to the procuring of lady subjects for our embellishments. In presenting our current number, we beg to express our gratification at having again been favored by the complaisance of our well-wishers. The young ladies whose portraits we give are the Misses Iona and Viola Misick, daughters of a well-known physician, residing in Sandwich, Illinois. Locally known as the "Twin Sisters," they have attached to themselves much interest from their strong personal resemblance, and the deceptions are numberless that they have been enabled to successfully perpetrate upon their relatives and friends.

The negatives were made at the establishment of Mr. Charles D. Mosher, in Chicago, and present specimens of good photography, in which no attempt has been made to produce ultra effects. We specially commend the manner in which the whites of the picture, represented by the sacques, have been rendered. Mr. Mosher was one of the unfortunate sufferers by the Great Fire [The Great Chicago Fire of 1871], but soon showed his enterprise by immediately afterwards building a new gallery. He has combined within it all the recent improvements, and uses his "Improved Skylight," an arrangement by which the upper glass sash can be elevated or depressed to suit the requirements of the time of day, or the necessities of the sitters.

Rev. Gilbert Small's Boys (Twins).
Harry S. Fetter, c. 1881, carte de visite.
Collection of James and Kathryn Abbe.

Wilbur and Wendell Johnson.
Lipp Studio, c. 1909, silver print.

Victor and Daniel Gorenstein.
Photographer unknown, 1932.

The Princes Richard and Christopher of Hesse (Twins).
T. H. Voight. Collection of James and Kathryn Abbe.

Twin Snowbirds.
Photographer unknown, c. 1893, stereogram.

Looking Down upon His Luck.
Photographer unknown, c. 1880, stereogram.
Collection of James and Kathryn Abbe.

Photographing the twins.

Photographing the Twins.
Artist unknown, c. 1885,
ink drawing.
Collection of James
and Kathryn Abbe.

The Value of Milk is Always Determined by its Quality.

*Advertisement for Curtis Babcock Milk
Test Machines.* c. 1905.

Alfred and Albert Smiley.
Lynn Revry, c. 1895, engraving from silver print.

View of Mohonk Mountain House, New Paltz, New York.

View of Minnewaska Mountain House Hotel, New Paltz, New York.

Twin devotion was a key to the success of Alfred and Albert Smiley. Born in 1828 and raised in the strict Quaker tradition, the Smileys were educators, until Alfred happened to take his family on an excursion into the mountains near New Paltz, New York, in 1869. Rounding a bend in the dense path, the group found itself facing a lake surrounded by rugged glacial rock. Alfred investigated ownership of the property and learned that it was indeed up for sale. With six children to support, he was in no position to consider purchase of the property, but wired his brother, saying, "Come immediately." Albert went, fell in love with the land, and soon raised enough capital to make the purchase. While Albert continued teaching in Providence, Rhode Island, Alfred, from his home in nearby Poughkeepsie, was able to set up a hotel operation, and by June 1870 the Mohonk Mountain House was open for business. In 1876 Alfred discovered another lake even grander than the first and built the Minnewaska Mountain House Hotel. In spite of strict Quaker rules that forbade card-playing, drinking, dancing, and traveling on a Sunday, both hotels were enormously successful, boasting such well-known visitors as Presidents Chester A. Arthur, Theodore Roosevelt and William Howard Taft. In place of those pleasures, the Smileys encouraged morning worship, contemplation and a generous helping of nature.

Today both hotels still stand, though the doors of Minnewaska have been closed and its structure is threatened with replacement by a modern hotel.

Mohonk Mountain House, however, still owned by the Smiley family, continues to function. Paul Goldberger, a *New York Times* writer on architecture, recently praised this historic house, with its huge fireplaces, overstuffed chairs, and flower-print curtains, saying, "It is like living in that grandmother's house we all imagine, without having to answer to a grandmother."

A guest who met Alfred Smiley in one of the long corridors of the house reportedly said to him, "I think it is foolish for people to say that they cannot tell you and your brother apart. Your expression is very different from your brother's, your eyes are darker and you are thinner." Alfred said perhaps he was right, then ran to the next stairway and reached the lower hall in time to greet the guest again, who said to him, "I just left your brother upstairs and told him how really easy it is to tell you and him apart. Your expression is different, your eyes are lighter and you are heavier." As a convenience to their friends, the Smileys facilitated identification by wearing different watch fobs.

Of his twinship, Albert Smiley wrote:

When my brother Alfred and I were born we were so much alike that our mother tied ribbons on either our arms or our legs, I do not remember which, to distinguish us. None of our neighbors knew us apart; we always worked together, walked together, slept together, had measles and mumps together; never had a single article of clothing or money or anything else separate for twenty-seven years. In the morning we jumped into the first suit of clothes that came in our way, no matter who wore it the day before. All our studies and reading were from one set of books, reading and studying simultaneously. Until we were twenty-seven years old, when my brother married, we had never had anything to be called "mine," but always "ours." At my brother's marriage we had to divide clothing and some other things, but till his death, four years since, we had many of our interests in common.

Francis E. and Freeland O. Stanley.
Photographer unknown, c. 1898.

It is no wonder Francis E. and Freeland O. Stanley had their picture taken when they completed their first "steam carriage" in 1898. They were photographers, with a prosperous portrait business, utilizing their own dry-plate process. Developing and building a steam car was a task they took on as a hobby after seeing what they considered to be an inferior model in 1896 at a county fair.

Unable to resist an invitation to enter their car in a speed and hill-climbing competition, they succeeded in setting a new world record and, as F. E. Stanley said, "In less than two weeks, we had received orders for over two hundred cars similar to the one shown there." The Stanley brothers had hardly any alternative but to become automobile manufacturers. Their cars continued to set records, putting gas-powered models to shame, but the twins were not interested in building an automotive empire. It is said that customers for the car were screened, as if they were applying for membership in an exclusive club. The Stanleys also stubbornly refused to advertise, believing that a good product could sell itself, and refused to mass produce, preferring to employ only the most skilled mechanics who built fewer than a thousand cars a year.

Probably because of such care, the Stanley Steamer was the fastest car on the road for years. In 1906, a Stanley Rocket set five world speed records, clocking 127.66 miles per hour. This was the first machine ever to go faster than two miles a minute. A year later, the same car became airborne at 197 miles per hour and crashed. The driver was thrown from the missile and seriously hurt, causing F. E. Stanley to decide "never again to risk the life of a courageous man for such a small return."

The Stanleys themselves, however, were not averse to letting out the throttle on the open road, and became well known for their frequent speeding violations. On at least one occasion, however, the brothers' twinship spared them a fine. A policeman, lecturing F. O. Stanley for his recklessness, was so stunned by the sudden appearance of an identical speeding vehicle driven by an identical person that he let both of them go.

In 1918, F. E. Stanley crested a hill only to find the road blocked by two farm wagons. Quickly he veered off the road, crashed into a ditch and was killed. Heartbroken, his brother sold their business and retired to Colorado, where he lived until he died of a heart attack at the age of ninety-one.

Maud and Michelle Bouvier.
Arnold Genthe, American, 1913, silver print.
Private Collection.

Lois and Lucille Barnes, in George White's Gay White Way.
Bruno of Hollywood, 1941.

Jeanette and Jean Kennelly.
The Chez Paree Adorables
in Chicago in 1936.

Beth and Betty Dodge in A Night
in Venice *at the Shubert Theater.*
"They whistle, sing and dance,"
Irving Chidnoff, 1929.
Billy Rose Theatre Collection.

TWINS NOW

Photographed by the Authors

Rocio & Yarmila

Rocio & Yarmila Aragon

Rocio and Yarmila Aragon are students at Sarah Lawrence College in Bronxville, New York.

YARMILA: We each chose the college we wanted separately.

ROCIO: When we realized we'd both chosen Sarah Lawrence, we said, "Oh, my gosh! How can we go to the same college?" And then we thought, just because we're twins, it doesn't mean we can't.

YARMILA: We decided to room together because we have our very particular habits. We're rather neat people. We get up really early in the mornings, anywhere between 5:00 and 6:00 A.M., and we go to sleep very late. We like to work out doing our exercises in our own room.

ROCIO: I like people. I like friends, and I don't like getting stuck in routines, but I *do* like doing certain things at certain times. And I know a lot of people can't cope with that.

YARMILA: We can cope with each *other* very well. We have our tiny, squibbles and squabbles, but not as much as we used to. We don't see each other so much now. We have very different schedules.

ROCIO: When we quibble, it's about small things, like, why put that bed over here? But inherently, we just get along very, very well. We always have. We have similar tastes, I'd say. But we've got very different characters. Once people get to know us, they say, "I would *never* have confused you two if I had realized how different you were."

My sister likes to be alone a lot, and I can't stand that. I'm generally more gregarious. I'm also more direct. People might say I'm a little bit colder than she is. My sister tends to be more open and I am a bit more reserved. I stay more aloof from people until I get to know them. But once I do, then I'm with them a lot more than she is. She's a little bit shyer, maybe. Also, we're less shy with women than with men, and we're less shy with older people than with younger people. She's a bit neater

Yarmila & Rocio

than I am—tidier. She can't stand anything lying around.

YARMILA: What people take to be shyness is actually a slightly softer way of dealing with them. I listen, but then I'll go away because I feel like being by myself, or ignore what's going on around me. It isn't really shyness; it's just a kind of distance. I tune out. I've got a much worse temper then she does and have to have a certain number of hours a day alone.

ROCIO: I really enjoyed this summer when I was working part time and taking a workshop, so I was around people thirty hours a week and the rest of the time, I was practically like a hermit.

YARMILA: I have wanted to dance since I was small, but we traveled around so much that I never really got to take classes. When I came here, I took the class to see what it was like and became completely absorbed. Luckily, we both seem to be flexible and to have the right kind of bodies for dancing. I'm more interested in ballet than modern dance, but not really classical ballet—more modern ballet.

ROCIO: I love dancing and I love to move, but I discovered that my strength and inspiration comes primarily from writing. My sister and I are hopeless about understanding economics, political science, things like that. We're both good at philosophy and literature, particularly.

YARMILA: I feel, between my sister and me, there's one part that's both of us. We're totally separate beings, yet it is there, it does exist, this oneness. It's a feeling of complete comfort and trust you know will always be there. Rilke talks about a kind of ideal relationship between two people—two spirits that touch and meet. And with twins, I think the touching and meeting is already there. It's the same principle. There is something which is both of us put together. Sometimes, my mother says, "Well, I've known you since you were babies, so I should know more about you than you know about each other." But we know that she just can't.

David & Christopher Alden

David & Christopher

Christopher and David Alden are directors of operatic productions. In 1979, Christopher made his debut with the New York City Opera, while, coincidentally, David was making his debut at the Metropolitan Opera.

CHRISTOPHER: The productions we did as children were inspired, that's for sure. They were great! We created fantasy characters for our younger brother. It was theater, heavy fantasy. We created a world with a whole mythology for him. To get him into fantasy and convince him it was true.

DAVID: We've been doing various theatrical events all of our lives. It never occurred to us that there would be anything strange or unreasonable or mistaken about going into the same profession. At the age of sixteen or seventeen, during our high school years, we both gravitated to opera and knew instantly that this would be the thing we'd stick to. Very few people in theater come to it late. Everyone connected with stage, with music, with opera, knows his chosen field at a very, very early age.

CHRISTOPHER: From a professional standpoint, the advantage of being twins has been having somebody there always from an early age to play off of—and being supported by the fact that there's two of us. We like to keep abreast of all the productions we're working on; it's mostly an exchange of information. The fact is that we're both so obsessed with the same profession. We're rivals in it to some extent, support rivals. This made us achieve things quickly. Our creativity is always being stimu-lated and fed by the other. I find it essential to always come back and discuss things with David. His reaction is more important to me than anyone else's.

DAVID: We don't work together at all. Nor do we really envision working together in the future. But we're always giving each other feedback, discussing productions in progress a lot, and we go to see each other's productions.

CHRISTOPHER: Just now I went to Glasgow to see David's *Rigoletto.* The problem was that I went backstage afterward. I was besieged by the cast and they refused to believe that I wasn't David. When I said, "I'm not David, I'm his brother Christopher," they answered, "You're joking!" I finally fled.

DAVID: We occasionally will observe the other at work. When I saw Christopher at work, it was very instructive to me. I've learned a lot watching him direct. It's very much like watching a mirror image of myself, at the same time I'm totally objective and distanced from it. I see my own mistakes right there. It's a rare opportunity not afforded people who don't have a twin.

CHRISTOPHER: People who are not twins find later in life the sort of relationship that we experienced at the beginning of our lives. It creates a power, having someone else there. You are not alone. You have someone to be supportive, so you are not worried about feeling isolated and alone—things many people tend to worry about.

DAVID: In our work, because there are two instead of one with the same artistic and esthetic goals, being a twin has a magical element of support and power.

Phil & Steven Mahre

Phil and Steven Mahre are champion skiers. They were photographed just hours after Phil won a silver medal for the United States in the 1980 Olympic slalom competition at Lake Placid, New York; they were interviewed shortly thereafter, the day after Steven won the slalom and placed second in giant slalom in national competition at Squaw Valley, California. They were raised on top of the ski slopes at White Pass, Washington.

PHIL: We started skiing when we were six and started racing when we were about eight, and we've just been at it ever since. We definitely do compete against one another, but it's not just Steven that I have to beat and it's not just me that he has to beat. We have to ski against the whole world. Really we don't have a big rivalry. When Steven wins, it makes me feel good. I feel if I can't do it, he may as well be the one. Keep it in the family.

STEVEN: When we were younger, he was my basic competition, and I think there was more of a rivalry between us then than there is now. Now there really isn't, because we have to beat so many other people out there. When I'm not doing well, I like to see him doing well. It's like he's part of me; I've grown up with him. At the Olympics I ended up falling, and knowing that he was leading was really good. It was really super to have him be ahead after the first run. And then he had a little trouble and ended up coming in second over all. Just knowing that there is an American able to do that well in skiing, and to have that American your brother is really a great feeling. We only had one fight in twenty-two years. I ended up hurting Phil and he started crying and that made me cry. We were about nine or ten at the time.

PHIL: We get along very well. Our only fights were about stupid little things, and that was when we were younger. Now we never fight. It's very weird. Sometimes it's like he's just an extension of myself. If I don't do well, I like to see him do well. When he wins, it's a victory for me, too.

Phil & Steven

Renee & Ramona

Renee & Ramona Rolle

Renee and Ramona Rolle are working on their master's degrees in petroleum engineering at Stanford University in Palo Alto, California, and hold summer jobs with Exxon. Their parents met and were married in Germany, where the twins spent their first seven years.

RENEE: Our parents were prepared for only one child. We were positioned so that when we kicked, we kicked at the same time, and our mother didn't know till she was on the table. She gave birth to Ramona and she thought she was finished, until the doctor said, "You're not finished, you have one more coming."

RAMONA: They had to go out and buy duplicates of everything really quickly.

RENEE: Ramona was always dressed in pink and I always got blue. All these little underwear and T-shirt sets.

RAMONA: We were separated for the first time in first grade. We had one best friend who was put with Renee. That really left me alone. I don't think I liked one day of that whole year. I couldn't wait until school was out so I could rush to their classroom and then go home and play with them. Later, at college there were times when it helped to have Renee there, like when I couldn't make a lecture because I wanted to get help with a problem, so she went in my place.

RENEE: I think twins should pool their strengths. While you can make use of it, you should use your twinship as far as you can. People remember you because you are twins so there is no reason in the world why you shouldn't take advantage of it and push yourself as far as you can. That is, if you feel you can work together and the work is equally distributed.

RAMONA: We only switched once and that was in a job interview. The job needed someone who could type sixty words per minute. She only typed fifty-five, so I took the test and I typed sixty-five with fourteen mistakes. She got the job.

RENEE: But I only kept the job for a few days because then I got the one I really wanted.

RAMONA: We weren't taking too big a risk because I was only there a half-hour or forty-five minutes. I don't really like doing things like that though. I mean most people can tell us apart.

A lot of guys we meet seem to think we just go together. They don't know, if they ask me out, whether Renee will come along. I received a Christmas present once from a boyfriend and he felt obligated to give Renee the same thing. They think we are so close it would be impossible to break it up. So we haven't had many dates and those we have dated have been remarkably different men. We are attracted to the same types of men, but different types of men are attracted to us, because we are different. She is the serious intellectual type.

RENEE: That's right. A teaching assistant in one of our classes gave an evaluation of our homework and said, "Renee is always quick, to the point and accurate, and Ramona always thinks in terms of theoretical what-if's." And I think Ramona has become more open. She used to be a very closed person. Now she listens and is a lot more open and more like me.

Jeff & Allan Kausch

Allan and Jeff Kausch were graduated from the University of California at Berkeley in 1979. Allan works in a Berkeley bookstore and Jeff works with a professional balloonist. They are adept at a number of physical activities.

JEFF: Winning is not that important to us. Since we are so similar, it's like competing against yourself—competing against someone who has the same sort of judgment.

ALLAN: Over the years, we have worked out ways of competing so neither one wins or loses that much. The end is more what you're doing at the time than who wins. We've gone through all the sports—racquetball, swimming, rock climbing, but we don't participate in team sports much, probably because the competition is not individualistic. There's too much reliance on the team. We probably amplify each other's abilities. If I go a little faster on a turn, then he knows he's capable of doing it too. When we were in judo, we could practice on each other. We're the same weight, the same height, and have the same abilities. We were evenly matched and that helped us practice.

JEFF: I cannot think of any one sport that I've done that he hasn't done. I may pursue a sport more or he may pursue one more. But we do most of them together. I would pick up something and he would follow.

ALLAN: And then I would go one step beyond where you'd gotten—a certain leapfrogging.

JEFF: He got hit in the eye with a badminton racquet and has an artificial lens, so that's one small difference.

ALLAN: My depth perception is off, so sometimes I rely on his judgment instead of on mine. I've been reading science fiction for a long time—it's one interest that is exclusively mine. There are things that are exclusively his. We sort of respect each other's areas so that we don't overlap.

JEFF: So that there is no comparison. Other people don't compare us. We don't compare ourselves or compete. And it's the same with our friends. We have a few, a handful of friends who know both of us equally well, and we have our own sets of friends. They find it difficult to be in the room with both of us together because we talk in stereo to them. It takes a rare sort of person to be able to talk to both of us at the same time.

ALLAN: A lot of people think of us more as twins and can't see us as individuals.

JEFF: I understand why people confuse us, but I still don't like being called Allan.

ALLAN: I don't like being called Jeff and being looked on as a set.

JEFF: They see me doing something, they automatically assume Allan is that way too. They see us as one personality, blended together and manifested into two people. My sister, or our sister, felt she was in competition with both of us. If she were to argue with one of us, she felt she had to argue with both of us. I guess we were more likely to side with a brother against a sister every time. That's how she felt her whole life, probably still does.

ALLAN: Being twins was a fact of life from the very beginning.

JEFF: I get the feeling that there aren't many boring twins. Because of the amplification or whatever they all seem to have well-developed interests.

Jeff & Allan

Tim & Tom Gullikson

Tennis players Tim and Tom Gullikson are ranked among the top ten doubles teams in the world. Before a roaring crowd at Wimbledon in 1979 Tim upset John McEnroe, who had been favored to win the title. With their easy grins, impeccable technique and unflappable personalities the Gulliksons have played their way to the top of the pro circuit.

TOM: Having a twin was an advantage in that I always had someone to play with—I never had to look around for a partner. I was about three or four when I realized that the person I'd been playing with looked like me. We started playing tennis when we were about five. We lived opposite a tennis court. And it was encouraging to have a twin, because I always thought, If you can do it, so can I.

TIM: People treated us special, because we were pretty good athletes.

TOM: One of our instructors called us Tim-Tom, because he could get either of us with that name. We have different games, different styles. He has a more aggressive personality. I have a more casual, laid-back personality.

TIM: I've always been a little bit more aggressive, more emotional. I always was the "holler" type of guy on the team. One problem with being twins is that people take it for granted that we will be willing to share. For example, on the circuit, we are given one car for the two of us when all the other players get one car each.

TOM: And they assume we will want to share a room. We don't like being introduced as "one of the Gullikson twins."

TIM: As far as being your own person goes, I resented being dressed the same. Our parents finally realized that we didn't enjoy it. If I were a parent of twins, I would not dress them alike. I would encourage independence in them—not to pursue the same interests but to do things on their own. I'd take each twin on separate outings and do things with each one individually. I think Tom and I probably spent too much time together.

TOM: Twins should develop separate interests, their own personal interests. If it differs from that of your twin, that's fine!

TIM: But most twins have a special bond of friendship that not too many people can understand.

TOM: It's very important to be tolerant and patient with people and their questions.

TIM: Tom and I were together really a lot, until our third year of college.

TOM: When I graduated from college, I took a job at Crystal Lake, Illinois, and Tim was in Ohio. It was the first time we were separated and we missed each other and visited a lot.

TIM: You can enjoy being twins once you know how to be your own person.

Tim & Tom

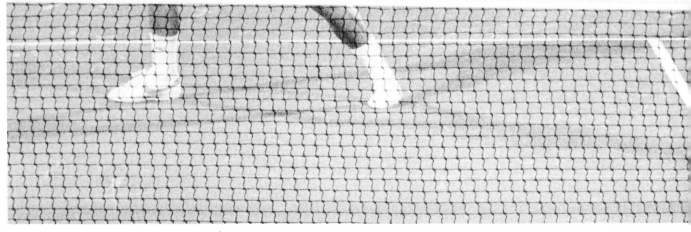

Genevieve & Eloise

Genevieve & Eloise Reed

This photograph was taken of Eloise and Genevieve Reed at the age of ninety-four in the pink lace dresses they wear when they ride in local parades. Today they live in the farm town of Lemoore, California. They appeared in the *Ziegfeld Follies* on stage, and in silent films for fifteen years. The early photographs were taken at the turn of the century.

GENEVIEVE: We sang all kinds of songs. "How You Gonna Keep 'em Down on the Farm, after They've Seen Paree." I sang that on the stage. "Over the River" with Eddie Foy. One was called "Old Town," in New York. We were with Charles Dillingham, our manager, and the *Ziegfeld Follies.* Ziegfeld and Dillingham took a lot of our publicity pictures. I mean before we went on the stage, to put us on the stage. We had a brother who just passed away a little while ago. He was three years older than we are. He was an actor. He had leading parts. He took us back east with him.

ELOISE: I'm older.

GENEVIEVE: She's five minutes older. My mother wasn't sure she was going to have another one. I was the surprise.

ELOISE: She wasn't sure she was going to have Genevieve. I was the firstborn. She said, "Do I have to have another one? Oh my God."

GENEVIEVE: We were born in Salem, Oregon. My grandmother crossed the plains in '49. We lived in Seattle and went to school there, and then they wanted us to go on the stage. Mother had a lovely figure. Father was older and he was adjutant general of Oregon. My mother gave us singing, dancing and art lessons. We did go to New York with a bunch and got in with the big shots. We're rather famous. We played with Montgomery and Stone. We played all over the South and the United States and Canada, Chicago, Cuba. One season in Cuba. And I got stranded there.

ELOISE: You missed the boat and I was worried to death about you.

GENEVIEVE: I had a beau in Cuba. He made me miss the boat.

ELOISE: A lot of rich guys fell in love with us, millionaires even. Once I had to learn a part in French. A Frenchman taught it to me word by word, but it was so long that I told Genevieve she would just have to learn the second half and go on in my place. She did, and no one ever knew the difference. Things like that happened to us because we looked so alike. People can't tell us apart. Of course we don't look as alike as we did when we were young.

GENEVIEVE: We're getting pretty old. I don't think many twins live this long, to be ninety. We're ninety-four this April.

ELOISE: I never tell my age.

GENEVIEVE: I've been in the movies. That was ages ago. *Last of the Mohicans.*

ELOISE: I didn't know you were a star in pictures. I didn't do as much as you did, and I never bragged about it.

GENEVIEVE: Twins have a right to fight. We were both in pictures. I rode on horses.

ELOISE: Now we manage to do our own cooking and that's about all we do.

GENEVIEVE: We're famous. We're twins. That's it.

Charles & Wilmer

Charles & Wilmer Frederick

Charles and Wilmer Frederick own and operate the Glendale Valley Farm in New Hope, Pennsylvania. The eighty-acre tract has been in the family since the turn of the century. The brothers live in sprawling ranch houses on either side of the original farmhouse where they were born.

CHARLES: On a farm you never have a duty just your own. You switch. There's plowing, harrowing, planting, feeding the animals, caring for them, milking. I pay the bills and Wilmer figures the tax at the end of the year.

WILMER: We once had an accountant, but decided to hell with it. We might as well do it.

CHARLES: On a farm, everyone works to survive. Helping in the field, working the hay, mowing. In addition to the one hundred twenty dairy cows, we raise and fatten a hundred pigs a year. We drop them off at the livestock market in Quakertown. When you're in the farming business, you can't let the animals become pets. The local dairy people have a nice cooperation. We have meetings together, discuss problems, the market, new ideas, money. Every other week I take one Sunday off. Otherwise, the hours are 5:30 A.M. to 6:30 P.M. and in the summer, the day goes on until 9:30.

WILMER: When we were kids, we used to go swimming before dark. Just clear the cows out of the creek and jump in. We went to a one-room school house till sixth grade. We graduated in 1940 with four other sets of twins. We always wore the same color shirts, pants and everything alike. We were both called "Fred" so nobody would call one of us by the wrong name.

CHARLES: In high school, we played all the sports— track, basketball, baseball and soccer. If war hadn't come along, we would have had the most letters. We were separated in the war— both in the Marines. They wouldn't let us both go overseas, because they didn't want to risk our both being killed. Afterward, we came back to the old homestead.

WILMER: I never did see another place I'd like to live better than here.

LaVelda Rowe & Arthur Richmond

Arthur & LaVelda   LaVona & Alwin

LaVona Rowe & Alwin Richmond

Identical twin sisters LaVelda and LaVona Rowe were wed to identical twin brothers Arthur and Alwin Richmond on June 5, 1976. They delight in their state of dual matrimony.

LAVONA: We often stop twins on the street to tell them about the International Twins Association and other twin clubs we belong to. One day in 1973, driving through Aurora, Illinois, to visit twin girl friends, we saw a set of identical twin brothers, dressed alike, walking down the street in step. Because of traffic, we couldn't stop.

LAVELDA: We felt that men their age, still dressing alike, would enjoy joining a twins club. Our girl friends told us that they had heard of "the twins who walked Broadway," but didn't know who they were and would find out. A few weeks later the girls called. After many phone calls, they'd found out where the twins worked.

LAVONA: We called the boys; Arthur answered. We told him about the twins club—and the next meeting in Springfield, Illinois. He was noncommittal, and we thought he wasn't interested. To our surprise, at the convention a set of heavyset twins came up and introduced themselves. We told them we were glad they decided to come and hoped they had a nice time. They walked away. Then both sets of us won the most identical contest in our age groups and had our picture taken together.

LAVELDA: Lavona and I were co-presidents of the Northern Illinois State Twins and were looking for secretaries. Arthur and Alwin agreed to take the jobs, so we saw them often. Then in September 1975 new officers were elected. We shook hands with the fellows and thanked them for a job well done. Arthur said "Just because we're not going to be in office together is no reason we can't see each other, if you want." We "wanted," and began accompanying them bowling and having dinner dates. In November, they proposed, in unison, on bended knees. And we answered, in unison. We got our rings for Christmas 1975, and we were married June 5, 1976.

LAVONA: The wedding was something out of a movie. We had thirty sets of twins present. Dad walked between us down the aisle. Our ring-bearer walked between a set of identical flower girls. It was truly a doubles day. The vows were in unison and the minister was so flabbergasted that during rehearsals he married Arthur to Alwin.

LAVELDA: In order to prevent a disaster during the actual ceremony, he had the names of the brides and grooms on the ring pillow. The photographer saw so many doubles he forgot half the pictures he should have taken. Twin bridesmaids, entertainers, flower girls, twins at the brides' book, at the cake, at the punchbowl, and as hostesses caused everyone to do a double-take. The only thing we couldn't find was twin ministers.

LAVONA: We double-honeymooned in Canada for two weeks. We got lost trying to find our hotel at 2:00 A.M. and got a police escort when we stopped to ask directions. One motel man was embarrassed about the four of us sharing a room, and hung a sheet between the two beds.

LAVELDA: We live together in a three-bedroom house in Aurora. We share a joint bank account, and own everything together. Wherever you see one set, you see the other. We are always together.

LAVONA: That the fellows look alike makes even us take a second look occasionally to be sure we're with the right one. If they grab and kiss the wrong wife, we just laugh and say, "Caught you there."

LAVELDA: The oldest of both sets—both are older by six minutes—are both left-handed. The youngest of both sets are right-handed. The oldest married each other and the youngest married each other. We have documented eighty-one sets of twins who have met and married twins. Of the eighty-one, we are the only known mirror-image twins to meet and marry.

LAVONA: We are twins first, individuals second. We believe we are being individuals by being alike, as we are doing what we really want, and not what society says we must do. By enjoying our twinship, we express our individuality.

LAVELDA: Arthur and Alwin were the thirteenth set of twins we dated. Guess thirteen is our lucky number.

Harriet and Beth Troxell are gymnasts, track stars and cheerleaders at the University of Alabama, looking forward to careers in the promotion and selling of sporting goods.

HARRIET: I really didn't realize how special we were until we took biology and studied identical twins and when the teacher explained it to us, I sat there and said, "Hey, Beth, we're kind of weird. We're freak accidents."

BETH: We went home and said, "Hey, Mom"—we had to check it out—"are you sure we're identical twins?" And she said, "Oh, yeah, the doctor said you all came from the same sac and you all were identical twins." And I said, "Do you know, Mommy, that we are rare?"

HARRIET: The main relationship both of us have had is with each other. Occasionally, we'll be apart because of summer jobs. You can't really know how it is to be a twin unless you *are* one.

BETH: But our parents have always treated us as sisters and individuals. They haven't really elaborated on the fact that we look alike. They never said, "Harriet wants this so Beth will want it too." We did dress alike but it was our choice. That's what outside people do not realize. They think somebody forces you to dress alike.

HARRIET: I remember when we were shopping for all these clothes that were alike, and I realized that we could have a wardrobe twice as big if we each bought different things.

BETH: And the minute we realized that we did *not* want to dress alike, we *didn't*. And Mother didn't say, "Come on and dress alike—you're so cu-ute." She never did that.

HARRIET: We have one older sister. I love her. During our childhood, though, instead of fighting with each other, we'd fight against our older sister. I mean, it was war! Us two against

Beth & Harriet

her. She's in grad school now. She's going into physical therapy.

BETH: We've lived together all our lives and we've learned that bickering never helps any situation. We know that one of us has to take the responsibility for each thing that we do, and it just kind of happens spontaneously. Neither of us, for instance, really likes to drive, so in driving to Tuscaloosa, we always alternate. We don't have to say, "I did it last time." It's kind of built-in.

HARRIET: There's a lot of mysterious things about twins, about being able to read each other's mind. A producer talked to us about a television series about twin detectives who can read each other's mind when they're in different places. Once in a while we will do that. One time, Beth was trying to think of the punch line to a joke but she hadn't told the joke yet, and I just called out the punch line

without having heard the joke. Everybody just stopped eating and looked at me. I didn't realize what I had done.

BETH: Being twins makes some things easier. Being cheerleaders, we have to work out, and it's always a lot better to work with a partner, and you always have a partner there.

HARRIET: Beth and I are fortunate because we really never have competed against each other except in gymnastics. A victory for her is a victory for me. If she beats me, I'm more thrilled than she is many times.

BETH: In tournament competition I try to compete only against myself. Otherwise you go bananas!

HARRIET: When you start competing against others you not only start competing physically, but mentally as well, and it really will drive you crazy. You should only compete against yourself. But if anyone has to beat me, I hope it's Beth.

Vivian & Marian

Vivian & Marian Brown

Vivian and Marian Brown spend their Sundays strolling favorite routes of San Francisco, dressed in carefully coordinated outfits, meeting passersby attracted by their absolutely identical appearances. They have been chosen "most identical" from among hundreds of other identical sets of twins at international conventions. They moved to San Francisco from their birthplace, Kalamazoo, Michigan.

VIVIAN: We just love hats. This hat is nice to wear on windy days. You don't have to worry about it blowing off. It will tip but it won't fall off.

MARIAN: We have had large straw hats. The one we picked last spring season has a large brim. It's shocking pink and it's decorated with daisies. We love shocking pink.

VIVIAN: What made us so interested in clothing was that when we were in college, we put ourselves through school and we wore plain white Ship 'n Shore blouses and black skirts. As soon as we started earning our own money, we started putting our outfits together.

MARIAN: We feel it is a blessing to be twins. Why take something that is a blessing and not make something of it?

VIVIAN: I think it's because we each have our own freedom. We do what we want as individuals and together. We don't feel we're giving up something for the other person. We do things because we both want to do them.

MARIAN: In being a twin, with share and share alike, it puts you in order for the human life you always have to live, because you can't always have your own way.

VIVIAN: It's a give-and-take matter.

MARIAN: Vivian walks me to work in the morning, because I have to be at work at eight-fifteen, and Vivian gets off from work fifteen minutes later at night, so then I walk over to meet her and we walk home together.

VIVIAN: I get my advantage early in the morning walking to work; the streets aren't as crowded. Then we meet for lunch. We go to a place where you can get your open-face sandwich, your coffee and dessert for $2.35. In the financial area you have to pay about that much just for a large sandwich.

MARIAN: Our money is pooled. If my sister gets a raise, it's like a little raise for me.

VIVIAN: Really, since we want the same things and buy the same things, everything is identical, so it costs the same for both of us. We know when we get to the end of our budget, which we often do, then we eat soup for dinner, and it's really healthy for you.

MARIAN: By splitting everything down the middle, we can each be a lady of leisure every other day. It's not that somebody waits on you or anything, but somebody gets your dinner and this is really good when you work all day. You really don't like to go home and think of something you can get for dinner that's quick, so this solves it. Half the time it's not bad, you see. We're what you might call part-time cooks.

VIVIAN: I'm paid every week so we more or less use what I make for our everyday expenses, and Marian is paid bimonthly so we use her money for rent because you need that in a lump sum.

MARIAN: And what's left over sometimes goes for bills.

VIVIAN: One of our favorite things is to shop. Oh, we love to go downtown to I. Magnin's on Saturday. People who sometimes come down say to us, "Didn't I see you here the last time I was here?" The best thing about being a twin is that you meet so many interesting people. I mean people feel like they can come up to talk to you, more so than just to anybody.

MARIAN: Particularly here in the city after we had that article which appeared in the *Examiner* in 1976 and then we appeared on that evening show and then also on that people show. They feel they have a certain amount of your background and . . .

VIVIAN: Then they think they know a little depth into what your life-style is.

MARIAN: And one man came up to me after he had read the article in the *Examiner* and he said, "I didn't know you worked." I said, "Oh, yes, I've worked all my life since I was sixteen."

VIVIAN: What do you pay your bills with if you don't work?

MARIAN: I always write the checks for the rent, that's always my obligation, and she writes the checks for the telephone company. Some things she takes over, some things I do. Our relationship is all on a voluntary basis. There is nothing that binds us legally or any other way.

VIVIAN: I always feel that blood is thicker than water.

MARIAN: Mother didn't dress us alike. And she didn't force us. It was all volunteer. Nothing should be forced.

VIVIAN: We have a hundred hats—fifty each. When we move, we have to make sure there's room to store the hatboxes.

MARIAN: We had twin Oldsmobiles in 1965. They were white with blue interiors—matching. They were twin cars, but they handled a little differently.

VIVIAN: We think twins are the only thing to be. We have known each other since we kicked in the crib.

Alan & Alvin

Alan & Alvin Chow

Alan and Alvin Chow are pianists at the Juilliard School of Music in Manhattan. They are from Miami, Florida, and were graduated from the University of Maryland, delivering a joint valedictory address.

ALAN: We started playing piano at age five. Our mother thought it would help our learning process develop before we got to school. We didn't decide on music as a career though until we were fifteen or sixteen.

ALVIN: I guess in the career of music, being twins has certainly aided us in being remembered. It's given us higher visibility, even though we don't play together often. We suffered in the beginning as a team because we were hiding each other's weaknesses. The sound of two pianos can cover up a lot of the subtleties, and so our solo playing was not very strong. So that's what we've been working on. We finally have reached the point where we're also strong as individual musicians, so that when we do put ourselves together as a team, we are not hiding anything; we're just adding to the total.

ALAN: Sometimes I think you can get away with things, knowing that the other person can take care of you if you don't want to do something. Alvin has this terrible thing about making telephone calls, so I do all the telephoning. But he's a better letter writer, so he does that.

ALVIN: Well, I guess I'm very dependent on him. It's a little difficult because all our lives we have always depended on each other. Our parents have instilled this in us. We find ourselves saying "we," or "our," when there's only one of us there, so it's confusing to a lot of people

if they don't know we have a twin. Now we're trying to separate ourselves just a little bit, being aware of our own separate identity. Until the eighth grade, we dressed alike. We had been fighting against the idea for a long time, but it was our brother who decided it was just terrible. He was in college, and at our birthday party he discussed the clothes question as a family matter. We have a very, very strong church background, and our parents felt there had to be something deeply significant about their having twins—two born at the same time. They're very keen about the both of us staying together for the rest of our lives, I think. On the phone this weekend, they said, "Whatever you do, you two stick together and make your decisions together."

ALAN: I think we're very different.

ALVIN: Very different. In temperament, I'm more like our mother and he's more like our father.

ALAN: We stopped studying together in eighth grade, too.

ALVIN: We just argued too much.

ALAN: It was very time-consuming.

ALVIN: People are always talking about the psychic communication between twins, but we've never experienced anything like that. I think the times we feel the same about something or sense something, it's just a matter of habit. I don't think there's anything extrasensory about it. People say we work very well together because we're twins. But again, our training is so similar that we tend to do the same things. I think because we look better on stage, the audience thinks we're going to play better too.

Andrea Gray is a projects organizer for the arts. She lives in New York City. Her twin, Adrienne Hines, chairs the board of the Arts Council in Richmond, Virginia. During a reunion in New York Andrea and Adrienne were photographed for these pages. The photographs on the following pages are from their debutante party in 1964.

ANDREA: I feel that I am a distinct individual from my sister. It has taken me to age thirty-five to finally arrive at that point, but I think now that I am just the same as any other individual human being. I have my own basic sense of security and my own sense of self. I like to be special and different—to be well dressed and be the center of attention—partly because I used to always be the center of attention by virtue of the fact that I had Adrienne along. When there are two of you, you are automatically unusual. Without the twin, you have to find some other way to be special in your own way. Ten years ago, I didn't have much sense of self. I hadn't detached from the twinship and therefore I was in need of someone I could be very dependent on in a mate. I finally got over that and realized that I don't need anybody else. I'm a whole person myself.

My sister got married first. She became engaged very quickly and she got married very quickly. I was very disappointed, and I didn't know how to cope with the fact that Adrienne was gone. Suddenly, I didn't have my identity. My sister was the other half of me. I was only fifty percent a person, and it was very hard to stand on my own two feet. I fell into a very dependent relationship soon afterward with a young man. I needed someone else to replace my sister. I didn't think of a career. I thought about a person, and I selected right away a person who met all the right qualifications. He was good-looking, came from a nice family, had enough money. I thought he was very interesting. I took one look at him and said, "This is it. I am going to marry this man." That

was about six months after she got married.

I think the statement that it takes a special person to marry a twin really depends on whether the twins have disengaged and established their own identity. I think maybe a lot of twins have not. I really was half a person; there was this empty feeling in the bottom of my stomach. I never discussed how I felt when Adrienne got married and left me. I was twenty-two, we were just fresh out of college, and I didn't have a job. Furthermore, she kept our apartment with all our furniture, so I had to move back in with my mother, and I felt cast out. It was much harder than either of us realized at the time because we were not very good at articulating our feelings. A strange thing about our twinship is that, however close we are, we are not good at communicating our feelings. That comes from the way we were brought up—to repress everything. She is the closest person I will ever know, just by virtue of the fact that we spent twenty-four hours a day together for the first sixteen years of our life, and that we love each other so much. But, on the other hand, we never talked about life, sex or our futures. I guess we did not feel the need. So I find that our relationship is lacking in some areas—areas of real communication.

Adrienne has really prospered, and is very happy in her role as a wife, mother and a leader in the community. She entertains beautifully, she dresses well and everybody adores her. I tried that and it did not work. My marriages have not worked and I have now gone in a different direction. Although Adrienne and I look alike, sound alike and love each other deeply, we are two incredibly different people. I think people are taken aback by twins. I always try to memorize which is which in twins because I remember how it affected me not to have people recognize me as Andrea, and say, "Oh, which twin are you?" But even I have a hard time sometimes.

I don't remember competing with Adrienne.

Andrea & Adrienne

Adrienne & Andrea

We were both very bright, and studying together for exams was very stimulating. To have somebody very bright to study with you spurs you on to do better things. On the other hand, if Adrienne got an A and I got a B, or if she won a swimming race and I came in second, I would be thrilled. If I did not win, the next best thing was to have Adrienne win. I have never been angry at Adrienne at an important level. Twins are the most special thing in the whole world. I have always thought you were incredibly lucky if you were a twin. It is a gift, the closest relationship, outside of maybe wife and husband, and it is lifelong. And I pity people who don't have that close relationship. The funny thing is that we have lived apart for fourteen years now, since we were twenty-two, and yet as soon as we get back together, it is as if there had been no time lapse in-between. We pick up exactly where we last saw each other.

Ruth & Daphne & Alicia

Daphne & Alicia Jang

Daphne Grace Jang and Alicia Joyce Jang were born January 4, 1979, in San Francisco. Their father, Alen Jang, is from Canton. Their mother, Ruth Jang, is from Hong Kong. The twins were photographed at the age of three and a half months.

RUTH: Our babies each have two names—a Chinese name and an American name. The Chinese custom is to give children beautiful names with meanings rather than name them for relatives. Daphne Grace is called Me-Yen, in English "Beautiful Grace." And Alicia Joyce is named Jon-Yen, which translates to "Praise Grace."

ALEN: We weren't surprised to have twins because we knew ahead of time. But when people would ask me how I was, I would stutter. What could I do? I didn't know how to answer them.

RUTH: Usually twins come early. "Get as much rest as you can," the doctor said, "and let them grow." But I worked until the last month. Just the day before the birth, I was X-rayed. One baby was up, one was down. My goodness, I thought, they're fighting to decide who is going to come out first. When they were born, one was five pounds, eight ounces; the other was four pounds, eleven and a half ounces. The doctor doesn't know whether they are identical or fraternal twins because there was one placenta and two sacs. They do look alike lots of times, but sometimes when you look at them, they don't look alike that much. I just have to see when they grow up.

ALEN: See what they want to do.

RUTH: They are individual persons. It's kind of cute when they're babies dressing them the same. But when they grow up, I'm sure they are going to have their own character and their own thing. If they want to dress themselves the same, it's okay with me. When they first came home from the hospital, they ate every three hours and on different schedules! Sometimes when this one is up and you feed her and then you go back to sleep, an hour later the other one gets up and then you go back again. All night. So now when one is up, we wake up the other and feed her too, so that they are both up at the same time.

ALEN: Many nights I have to get up in the middle of the night. I don't know which end is up. I have to take a deep breath. Both are crying together sometimes. You just have to keep cool. It's real tough.

RUTH: My mother really takes a big load. Sometimes when they both cry, you really need two people to do the feeding. Sometimes we really need two people at home. Now they sleep six hours through the night. Before they were up every three hours. It's better now. We try to put them to bed about ten o'clock so they can sleep a little longer. They usually get up at about four or five.

ALEN: We try to make the last feeding as late as possible and let them sleep through the night.

RUTH: My husband's family was so excited. They don't have any twins in their family and there are lots of boys. Just a few girls, you know. When the twins were both girls, they were so pleased.

Jeff and Bruce Ellis are vice-presidents of Ridgewell's, a family catering business in Washington, D.C., which has served the White House since 1928.

JEFF: In business, when you say "twins" you say "double coverage." During a party at the home of the ambassador from Morocco, the ambassador kept seeing me go to one side of the house to check on platters of hors d'oeuvres and Bruce go to the other side—back and forth and back and forth. After a while, he says to me, "My God, I never saw anybody move so fast in all my life."

BRUCE: When we were in seventh grade, I woke up one morning and didn't feel good. Jeff said, "Ha! He doesn't want to take the exam." I stayed home. Later, my mother had to call an ambulance and I went to the hospital. My appendix was about to burst. At school, Jeff, not knowing anything, started to get severe stomach cramps and had to spend the day in the infirmary.

JEFF: This television talk show we did. We had not discussed how we were going to dress or anything. He came in—same suit, tie, socks and shoes. You know, he'll buy a suit unbeknownst to me and the very next day I'll go out to buy a suit from a different salesman in the same store, and it will be the same suit.

BRUCE: My parents would dress us exactly the same. And we went around like namby-pamby cute little twins.

JEFF: Well, that wasn't too long.

BRUCE: That's what I'm saying—until we were about twelve. And everybody used to gawk and stare and you would feel as if you were on exhibit sometimes.

JEFF: But if you had twins, you would do the same thing.

BRUCE: I probably would. We're wearing the same uniform today. It's a lot of fun. In fact the other day I was shopping with my wife and a lady friend of Jeff's came down the escalator and gave me a big hug and kiss. My wife looked at me and I said, "I'm not Jeff, Mrs. Brown."

JEFF: Bruce used to date some dogs in college, and I would go down and say I was Bruce.

BRUCE: They weren't too bad! Otherwise Jeff wouldn't have gone down.

JEFF: One girl said, "Gee, you kiss much better than Bruce."

BRUCE: That last statement I don't think is tremendously accurate. But he did take her out twice while I was away. I went to the dorm and I said, "Where is so-and-so?" and they said, "You just took her out," and I said, "Son of a gun." So I got back in my car and went to find them. The girl couldn't believe there were two of us because I had never mentioned it to her. People used to call us "dittos," "carbon copy." Now we get Mutt and Jeff, because of Jeff's name. They say, "You must be Mutt."

JEFF: Whenever I saw Bruce, I ran the other way. I didn't like people gawking at us as if we were freaks or something. Life would be very dull and boring if everyone were the same. If Bruce were my exact clone it would be terrible. We are different. I'm more of a joker. I like to see reactions in people. I'll throw pies into their faces and send weird-looking cakes. We served this unbelievable formal dinner and I came up with this huge pewter turtle. I lifted off the top and there was a McDonald's cheeseburger and French fries. Then everyone got up and clapped. That's bringing people together, letting people enjoy themselves.

BRUCE: As long as I don't get blamed for his mistakes and am only complimented for the good things, I don't mind being his twin.

Bruce & Jeff

Peter & Paul

Peter & Paul White

Peter and Paul White are seniors at Yale University. Peter, a history major, plays varsity football. Paul is interested in ethnology and sociology and plans to attend law school.

PAUL: Peter didn't want us to go to the same school—he was dead set against it—but we decided if we got accepted at Yale, we could because we wouldn't have to room together. We didn't get assigned to the same college, so we live a block and a half from each other. I think twins can get tired of each other no matter how much they really love each other. You tend to rely on each other too much. I only applied to three schools and Peter only applied to two. I guess we were either overconfident or foolish. Twins are very confident people. Just knowing there's someone else like you, you tend to feel that no matter how much wrong you do, there is going to be someone to back you up. I would almost say it's a mystical thing—I feel that I can do no wrong. My brother is always supporting me.

PETER: Paul has always been extroverted and kind of sassy. When we were in different classes in first grade, he got in trouble and his teacher was going to make him stay after class. But he headed out the door anyway, and she grabbed him by the arm. I came along then and grabbed the other arm. "He's going with me," I said.

I mean, we are kin. I don't care whether the teacher was right or wrong. He was my brother. We were sort of precocious and always getting into fights with other little kids.

PAUL: When we see people now, they say, "I can't believe how nice you guys turned out to be. You were so bad as kids." I guess we were. Everything is exaggerated when you're that noticeable—being twins.

PETER: They called us "Thunder 'n Lightning." I'm glad that nickname went by the wayside. And they called us "Pete and Repeat," or sometimes "Peter-Paul." My dad didn't really know us apart. Anytime we did anything bad, he'd put us both over his knee and spank us at the same time. My mother said we had our own language. Once when we were about three, we said we wanted a "doo-ah-doo-ah" and a "nanga-nanga" for Christmas, and they couldn't figure it out, and we cried and cried. It turned out it was a guitar and a saxophone.

PAUL: Everyone finds it difficult to understand the way that twins can communicate with each other. I had a freshman counselor who said when he was in the same room with me and my brother that there was no way he could get a word in. Not that we talk only to each other. It is just that nobody can follow our conversation. Sometimes all it takes is a shrug and we both understand completely.

Mario & Aldo Andretti

Auto racing's twins, Aldo and Mario Andretti, knew from childhood they wanted to race. In their native Italy they worked as mechanics but longed to race cars, not to fix them. "There's one thing about winning a race," says Mario, "you never get used to it. Every time it's like the first time." When the twins were fifteen, the Andretti family emigrated from Italy to Nazareth, Pennsylvania. The day after they arrived in their new

Mario

hometown, the boys spotted a racetrack. When they entered the local races they could afford the fee for only one driver's license which, as twins, they shared.

Both were daredevil drivers, and are pictured at age nineteen in Nazareth with their first race car. Says Mario, "In racing you first learn to go fast and stay in one piece; then you learn to drive." In 1969, the year Mario won the Indianapolis 500

race, Aldo's second serious racing accident convinced him to retire and he decided to build an automotive supply business. He is president of the Associated Sales Corporation in Indianapolis, Indiana, which the brothers co-own. Mario continues to dominate the racing field. Nineteen seventy-eight was a record year for him with a series of victories; most notably, he won the world championship, the second American ever

Aldo

Mario & Aldo

to have won this honor. While they no longer travel the racing circuit together, the Andrettis vacation each winter with their families in the Poconos, where Aldo and Mario madly race each other in snowmobiles. "One has to beat the other," says Aldo. "And it's always a race to go nowhere."

ALDO: We were born in 1940 in Italy at the beginning of the war. We were born at home. There was a midwife and the doctor. The doctor delivered my brother first, and my mother —I found out twenty years later—was about to expire, and my father was losing his wits. "What's going on here?" The midwife said, "She's having a set of twins." The doctor said, "No! I only heard one heartbeat," and six hours later, I was born. It was just nip and tuck with my life, you know. When I was young, I sort of resented being a twin. I wanted individuality. I didn't mind being called Mario, and his being called Aldo—that became a way of life. But my mom always dressed us alike. I mean, we had the same shoes, the same this, the same that. And you know something? I wouldn't wear Mario's shoes, or his socks or his shirt or his pants to save my soul, and they were the same size and the same color. Neither would he wear mine. There was always a mutual understanding there. He didn't want to wear my clothes and I didn't want to wear his. I could always tell the difference. I don't know how.

I think we are more proud today of saying we are twins than we were then, because it was so tiresome. "Oh, my God! Look at these two boys. Like two drops of water. How can your mom tell you apart?" I used to hate the first day of school with the teacher—"Hi, John. Hi, Joe. And what do we have here?" I didn't want to be singled out. We shared the same girl friend when we were kids. Always one girl friend between the two of us. One little truck. We never had two of anything. One, to share.

We always avoided fighting. I criticize him for what he does and he criticizes me for what I do and we reach a compromise. That's all. So much between us is understood but not spoken. Neither one would have to ask for help. If the help were needed, I would be there. Maybe he's the only person with whom I am totally unselfish. And I just love to see him win, make money and be successful; and I think, likewise, that he loves to see me be successful. And the more successful, the happier he is.

Amy & Ann McCandless

Amy and Ann McCandless are twenty-year-old models for the Eileen Ford Agency. They are considering modeling in Paris, where it is more relaxed, "with two-hour lunches."

AMY: As twin models, Ann and I work together. We work well because we blend somehow and we don't push and shove each other like some of the other girls we see posing for photographs.

ANN: We love being twin models, because we show that twins can get along together.

AMY: It is important for people who look at our photographs in the magazines to sense that we know each other and that we are not strangers thrown together for the moment.

ANN: Amy and I discuss the power of being twins often. It's eerie and frightens us, but at the same time, we're convinced we'll get everything we want in the end. We think we're very lucky.

AMY: We rarely quarrel. If we do have a quarrel, we have it out in a few minutes and then say, "What shall we do next?"

ANN: It's not really an argument ever. Afterward one will say in a soft voice, "Fight's over," and we're friends again.

AMY: Part of being twins is dividing chores.

ANN: Amy is good at math and keeps track of expenses and banking. I'm lazy about money.

AMY: And I'm lazy about the phone.

ANN: When we're in a highly emotional or hectic situation, we take turns worrying. One is always carefree, the other does the worrying.

AMY: One gets an unplanned holiday from worry until the other says, "Stop being such a lazy twin. Now it's your turn. You make this phone call," and the roles reverse. And that wraps it up until the next worry comes along.

ANN: Twins are more secure because there is always someone there.

AMY: You see, twins can't be alone. They always have to have one person very close to them. When you have a boyfriend, he has to be as close to you as your twin was because you are used to a very close relationship.

Amy & Ann

Ann & Amy

ANN: So your husband or boyfriend replaces the twin that you've left.

AMY: You have to marry someone who doesn't mind that you're going to be around him twenty-four hours a day. No secrets. Some people can't handle that.

ANN: The only time we split up is when we shop.

AMY: And we go our separate ways on weekends.

ANN: In fact, if we're invited to a party and the host says "Bring your twin if you want," we'll sometimes say to the other, "You've been invited, but don't come because I want to meet more people." When there are two of us, we don't meet as many people.

AMY: Sometimes when one of us dates a new person we don't introduce the other twin to him for a long time. When finally we tell them we have a twin, they can't believe it. They can't wait to meet her.

ANN: You are treated differently then.

AMY: You lose your identity if you bring your twin around. The person will forget that you're the one he's supposed to be going out with.

He'll just have a good time and laugh with both of us. He might even go after the other twin if you're not careful!

ANN: Well, usually the twin who's been introduced later knows that she has to make herself a little less noticed. She can't outshine her sister in front of her sister's date.

AMY: The person is always going to be interested in what the other twin is like. You know, "Did I pick the wrong twin?"

ANN: Some people are lazy and don't make an effort to tell one from the other. "Here, Twinnie." It's terrible.

AMY: I think people feel they are coming up against an alien wall when they meet us. Especially because twins can signal each other with their eyes.

ANN: People always think that we're talking about them and playing games. "What are you two looking at each other like that for? You're talking about me, aren't you?" Well, no, we're not.

AMY: We're just looking at each other and saying with our eyes, "Are you having fun?"

Paul

Dick

Paul & Dick Sylbert

Paul and Dick Sylbert have had long careers in film production design. Paul has worked with the Metropolitan Opera Company and on fifteen films. Dick, a former vice-president of Paramount Pictures, has worked on twenty-three films.

PAUL: It was the Depression. Dick was born. About twenty minutes later, my father called my grandmother and said, "There's another one on the way." My grandmother said, "Oh, my God, I hope one of them dies." How do you like that for a first start?

DICK: There are pictures of us at three or four on a farm in New Jersey. We moved there right after the Depression. In ninety percent of the pictures, I'm standing on the right and he's standing on the left. When we get together, we just seem to get into that position.

PAUL: Everything was smooth until we were fourteen. Then we had two years of solid fights which our mother had to break up all the time. We were ready to kill each other.

DICK: The advantage of being a twin is the novelty of belonging to a small group of attention-attracting people. Being noticed never hurts at first. The problem is later on, of course, the separate identity problem. I think twins often play or choose different roles—good guy, bad guy, responsible, irresponsible, married, single—in an effort to be separate . . . and often reverse the roles from time to time. I think twins have to do this. The best thing twins can do for themselves is separate as much as possible. Twins who cannot separate can become monsters.

PAUL: As young kids, there is an immediate social identity as "the twins." Then you start to seek out individual lives. You begin to realize that you represent each other in such a strong way, and if you disapprove of something your brother is doing, you disapprove because it reflects on you. It's a package deal. It really is guilt by association.

DICK: It seems to me that twins can get along best by *patience.* After all, being twins isn't something one chooses. I think single individuals concentrate on the similarity between twins, especially identical twins. Twins, on the other hand, concentrate on the differences—being more familiar with the similarities.

PAUL: We went to Temple Tyler School of Fine Arts, and we got thrown out at the same time, when we were juniors. We could have gone to Florence to study, but I said, let's stay here and be painters. I got married, and my wife and I decided to stay in New York, and my uncle persuaded us to be scenic painters. I went with the Met as an apprentice. He went to NBC and painted scenes for TV. He was wearing Brooks Brothers gray and carrying a briefcase, and I was all covered with paint. He said, "You gotta try it." I went over to NBC and they hired me. I was now in the position of being confused with my brother, which had happened before but not in a long time. That kind of situation no longer suited us so, after three months, I went to CBS. He did all the big shows at NBC. He did wonderfully. Later I started to freelance and got a job with MCA (Music Corporation of America). Then a designer came and asked me to do a movie with him. I said I can't—do it with Dick.

DICK: Later Elia Kazan wanted me to do a film called *Baby Doll,* and I said, "If I do it, I'll do it with my brother." So Kazan hired us both to do *Baby Doll.* Then we did *Face in the Crowd.*

PAUL: We were always able to divide the work right knowing who had talents in what direction. A lot of shorthand goes on between us. We don't have to say a lot. I can get the whole message by the tone of voice.

DICK: We talk at length about fishing, which we both love, and about anything that doesn't have to do with work or really personal things. On the level of work or personal things, very little language is needed.

PAUL: I always felt that twins had the possibility of being each other, in a funny kind of way.

Elane and Eileen Arias were photographed at the age of three, with their sisters, Jennifer, four and a half, and Denise, five months. Their parents, Julio and Elsa, are from Santo Domingo.

JULIO: We didn't know twins were on the way until the first one arrived, Eileen. There was a flurry for a minute that there might be a third. I was downstairs in the lobby when the nurse told me, "You have two beautiful girls." "Oh, my God," I said, "two more girls!" Jennifer, the firstborn, was a year and a half when the twins were born. Two new babies crowd the older child, so I kept my time for her and tried to include her and to deal with her feelings and needs for affection and attention. Always I help a lot—taking care of the baby—I'm used to all that. It is easy to tell the twins apart. They have different foreheads. Elane is physically stronger than Eileen. Eileen is the more quiet, more deliberate. They love each other. All the time they look for each other. They have separate beds, but they don't use them. They twine together all the time.

Eileen & Elane

Julio & Elsa & Elane & Eileen & Jennifer & Denise

Ilia & Peter Kondov

When they were four years old, an older brother held them up before a mirror. "You are twins," he said, *"bliznaci."* Bulgarians Ilia and Peter Kondov made their United States debut in 1979 with the Ringling Brothers and Barnum & Bailey Circus. They started their careers in 1948, at the age of nine, when their father moved his own acting talents under the big top. The boys developed a bicycle act on the high wire, which they have been performing together since 1972. Peter balances his wife on top of a thirty-foot perch pole, which is balanced on his head, while he rides his bicycle across the wire. Ilia rides across with both wives pyramided on his shoulders. One night Peter thought he'd like to perform their final trick with the wire at a slant. His brother walked up to him and said, "You know what I'm thinking?" The answer, was "Yes."

Ilia & Peter

Samuel and Emmanuel Lussier were born August 11, 1877. They are listed in the 1978 *Guinness Book of World Records* as being North America's oldest set of twins, at age one hundred. They were photographed at Emmanuel's home in Northbridge, Massachusetts, where Samuel was visiting from his home in Cumberland, Rhode Island.

SAMUEL: When we were young there weren't so many twins as we have today. We were always dressed alike. Our mother tied pink and blue ribbons around our fingers to tell us apart. Whenever she called one of us and it wasn't the one she wanted, we'd say, "It's not me, Ma." That's the only way she could recognize us. We tried to play her tricks too. Now the only difference is Emmanuel is missing his appendix. It was on January 5, 1917. I know. I took him to the hospital January 3. We never had any argument. We never had a fight. We just wrestled to see who could be best. He was the best ball player. Oh, he could knock a ball. He made a hundred home runs and we won all the time. I played shortstop and second base. We played with Napoleon Lajoie and Jess Birkett. Emmanuel always followed sports more than me. He was always on the Yankees side.

When I was twelve, I worked in the mill, painting the ends of yarn bobbins for $2.05 for a sixty-hour week. It wasn't much, but if you didn't do it, you starved. I'd take home my pay packet and Ma'd give me back a nickel for a bag of peanuts. You have to be happy with what you're given. We married girls from the mill where we worked. Sometimes on the bridge, I'd meet his girl after work and we'd talk and she thought it was him, and all the time it was me. I got married in 1900 and he got married in 1901. He brought up a family of ten and has forty-two grandchildren, thirty-four great-grandchildren and five great-great-grandchildren. I have four children, three grandchildren and six great-grandchildren. Our family is small compared with his. God gave me a million in good health. Look at my face. No wrinkles to speak of. Many men younger than me are all wrinkled. And I still have quite a bit of hair on my head. I never worry. And I always said that if you speak bad about people, they'll speak bad about you. So I just think nice things. I never smoked and I never drank, because I think they're bad. And I never touched butter—that's bad for the liver. I'm home now. Home is where my twin brother is.

Samuel & Emmanuel

Nell & Kate

Nell & Kate Hirschman-Levy

Nell and Kate Hirschman-Levy were born December 4, 1979. They were photographed fourteen days later, and their parents, Jane Hirschman and Richard Levy, of New York City, were interviewed two months later

JANE: In my tenth week of pregnancy, I had symptoms of miscarriage. I was sad and upset. They sent me in for a sonagram. The technician flipped on the videotape and said, "You can look now." I saw what looked like a little shrimp, and I said, "What's that?" and she said, "That's a healthy baby," and I said, "What's that next to it?" And she didn't say anything. So I said, "Is that my fibroid tumor?" "No," she said, "that's another healthy baby," at which point I started crying hysterically, and Richard started crying too. The two of us were in tears, and I was gasping for air, and the technician kept saying, "Calm down, calm down." She said, "It's wonderful. It's two healthy babies." And the more she said the number "two," the more hysterical I got. And Richard was crying because he was so happy that everything was fine and he felt doubly blessed. She left us alone, saying, "Please stop crying. I'd like you to see the doctor, but you can't go in to him crying."

RICHARD: It's really very eerie to think back to that day. I can't believe it when I see these big chubby kicking babies. It was a very, very emotional experience. During the pregnancy it became very important for them to be twins. We started to talk about them constantly as two.

JANE: If someone had said, "You are going to have only one child," we would have had to mourn the loss of the other.

RICHARD: I'll tell you what is hard on the father—the total focus on the mother. Suddenly in our community of friends it was, "Jane's having twins." For the first time, I felt like someone trailing behind a celebrity. They'd ask Jane a hundred questions and I'd sort of stand by. But the first weeks after the twins were born, I really tuned in to them. I'd hold them, turn them upside down, undress them, look here and there, kiss them, feel them, smell them—all the things that you can do with new babies. The biggest problem was to avoid treating them as interchangeable. We'd forever ask one another, "Who are you holding? Who do you have?" "I have Nell." "I have Kate."

JANE: We haven't yet confused them and given the same one a bath twice. I think we're doing pretty well. But I also see how kids can get typecast very quickly. Already we're saying, "Oh, Kate, she's got the temper." She's the one, you know, who has to be pleased right away or she'll yell. The problem with twins is that you tend to compare.

RICHARD: At this point, though, it's less comparing than just trying desperately to find the individuality of each child. We do a night feeding together. We both get up and each take a baby. We warm up two bottles. We usually sit on the living room couch. The room is dark—we don't turn on the lights. It's very peaceful and quiet as we sit with the little babies. It's a very warm time for us. Jane and I talk a little, or just look at each other. We feel very close to each other at this time and close to the babies.

JANE: Someone asked in the elevator the other day, "Which is the mother?" Remember what you said?

RICHARD: We're all mothers.

Faye and Kaye Young are professional basketball players, playing forward position for the New York Stars. They are the daughters of Mr. and Mrs. Claude R. Young and were born in the rural community of Bunn, Franklin County, North Carolina. They star in a Dannon Yogurt television commercial.

FAYE: We first became interested in sports in seventh grade. At that time we were tall for our age, and someone asked us . . .

KAYE: If we would like to play on a junior high basketball team. And we walked on the court and fell in love with it.

FAYE: We played on junior high and high school teams and then we both received athletic scholarships to Peace Junior College in Raleigh. It's a small private college for girls—five hundred girls.

KAYE: And then we went to North Carolina State University our junior and senior years on scholarship. Our mother came to all our games in college.

FAYE: We graduated in 1978, and here we are.

KAYE: We decided to play the professional league, which has just been established. We both play forward.

FAYE: It's best when we're both on the floor. We enjoy that the most.

KAYE: Because we have a sense of knowing where the other one is, what she does best and where she wants the ball.

FAYE: Yes, and she'll help you out in defense.

KAYE: We can kind of read what the other one is feeling. You know, emotionally, I think we communicate without speaking.

FAYE: There's like a sixth sense.

KAYE: Little things like when Faye's not having a good game, or whatever, I always know without her having to . . .

FAYE: Everybody knows.

KAYE: I didn't mean it that way. Just that I know what you're feeling inside. We've always been pretty much on the same level as far as our skills are concerned.

FAYE: We've always participated the same amount of time and done the same things and have progressed the same.

KAYE: The very first question we get from reporters is, "Who has the better talent? Who is the better player?" And we always say, you know, it just depends on the time and the situation.

FAYE: Sometimes she plays better than me.

KAYE: You're better at some things and I'm better at others.

FAYE: We were the first twins born in a new hospital in our county, and people sent in suggestions of names. Everybody heard about it.

KAYE: Our mother wasn't expecting twins.

FAYE: We were to be the last baby. She had no idea.

Faye & Kaye

Paul and Peter Frame are dancers with the New York City Ballet company. They are from Morgantown, West Virginia.

PAUL: Peter came to New York first, in 1975. I hadn't made up my mind yet and I wanted to try college. I was with the Ohio Ballet at the time so I enrolled in the University of Akron. And that proved to be very hard. I hated doing two things at the same time. So, after a lot of searching, I decided I wanted to dance. I finally came to New York in the fall of '77.

PETER: He came to visit me. I brought him in and sat him down in a corner while I was getting dressed. People came up to him and said, "What's wrong? Are you injured or something?" because he wouldn't say hello to them. He wouldn't say anything. When I brought him in to the studio and—I hadn't told anybody that I was a twin—there was an unbelievable reaction. Sixty people said it was the best thing that ever happened.

For a while I think it was good for us to be separated because we had been so close for so long. We were together until the twelfth grade and, in a way, we took each other for granted. Later, at eighteen, nineteen, twenty, a lot of

things can happen. Those are important years to experience things for yourself. We both experienced them differently, and I was glad for that. I think I started knowing myself better. Now I appreciate more our being together.

I think probably our personalities are the way they are—happy and positive—because we're twins. We had a sense of security when we were younger. I needed Paul a lot. I've found now that I like being on my own.

PAUL: Lately, we both have different interests, but we like to see each other every once in a while. We have some good friends, wonderful people whom we go out and enjoy ourselves with. And they enjoy us.

PETER: They enjoy our being twins.

PAUL: One thing that used to bother me was when people pretended not to know who we were when they really did know. The whole thing about not being able to tell twins apart is fun for people. What makes me angry is when they know and they do it anyway. That bugs me. And the ordeal you go through when you're in a new place and everyone has to get used to the idea of twins.

PETER: Yeah, that's true. I want people to view us as individuals.

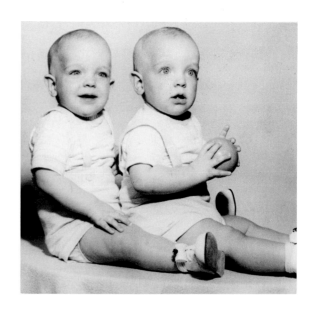

Paul & Peter

Marilyn & Rosalyn

Marilyn & Rosalyn Borden

Marilyn and Rosalyn Borden are singer-dancer-comediennes who have appeared on numerous coast-to-coast network television shows and have toured nightclubs across the country. They also do comedy emceeing and spent two weeks cheerleading for the San Francisco Bay football team, the Globe Gallopers. Marilyn lives in Newark, California, and Rosalind lives nearby in Hayward.

MARILYN: This is such a riot. We haven't done cheerleading before, but this is a comedy football team. Our team always wins and actually aside from being cheerleaders, we run the touchdowns and we carry the stretcher out on the field.

ROSALYN: So we do a little bit of everything.

MARILYN: And the cheers we do are standard cheers, like, "Go, team, go." And we play disco music and dance. Now we got an offer from a semi-pro football team to be their cheerleaders for their season starting the end of June. It's right in this neighborhood. We're willing to travel, but we try not to during our TV season because the uppermost thing in our minds is the TV season. They start taping in June or July. So we try to go to L.A. in June.

ROSALYN: When we're in L.A. we dress alike because it's good for business. But when we go to rehearsals, we don't.

MARILYN: As kids, we always had to be dressed the same, even to go to the grocery store. It was silly, ridiculous, and in a way, very sad.

ROSALYN: Not really. I mean we grew up in spite of all that. Now sometimes we dress differently but put the same earrings on or same top, by chance. It really is crazy.

MARILYN: We're a team. We love to work. We started when we were five years old on Ed Begley's "Children's Hour" on WTIC radio, Hartford, Connecticut, and later came out to L.A. When our father moved us, he got us on the "Spike Jones Show" and "Martin and Lewis" and he got us with Jimmy Durante. We worked with Jimmy for six years. We even got into his nightclub act.

ROSALYN: Then we semiretired for eight years after Marilyn got married. Not because she got married but because our business changed, and I had to make a living for myself out in the regular world. I call it the "straight" world. I went to Los Angeles and worked there for five years and now I've been back for three and a half years.

MARILYN: We hated it.

ROSALYN: It was more traumatic for Marilyn. She couldn't adjust to me being away. I adjusted better than she did. Everybody thought I would be the one to fall apart, and I didn't. Marilyn did.

MARILYN: Well, I really didn't fall apart, but I missed the business. I missed Roz being near me. It was not enough for me just to be married. We love to work together.

ROSALYN: So I came back.

MARILYN: And I'm glad she did.

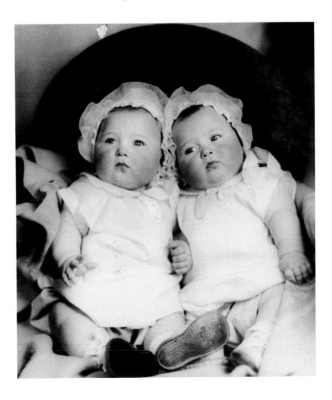

Leslaw & Waclaw Janicki

Leslaw and Waclaw Janicki perform with Poland's avant-garde theater group, the Cricot 2. The troupe, which is well known throughout Europe, made its first American appearance in 1979 in *The Dead Class*. Photographs of that performance are on the following pages.

WACLAW: Being twins is not a matter of magic; however, we believe we have more luck than others. So far, our life has unfolded happily.

LESLAW: Twins are more open to other people, so people are pleased to have them around—although sometimes there is some resentment from others, and some look at us as an aberration of nature.

WACLAW: Personally, I never feel that I have an identical twin brother. I see emotional differences between us although outsiders view us as similar. But physical appearance is nothing. From our point of view, we are two different individuals at heart, but we would do anything for each other. There is no doubt that twins are emotionally closer to each other than any other siblings. Thus far the events of our lives show how close we are to each other.

LESLAW: Somehow it happens in our lives that we end up doing things together. We made our decisions together. What two heads can do, one cannot.

WACLAW: Togetherness is our destiny.

Leslaw & Waclaw

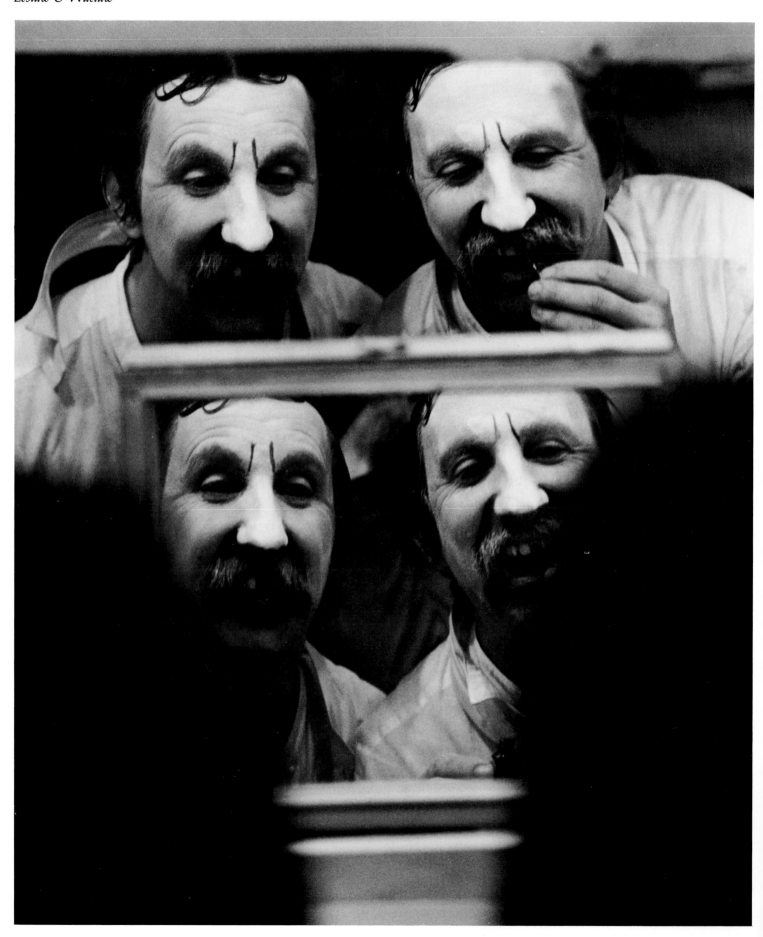

The Janickis in scenes from the 1979 La Mama production of *The Dead Class.*

Jessica & Amy

Jessica & Amy Reid

Ramsay and Betty Reid are the parents of Ramsay, four, twins Amy and Jessica, six, and Jennifer, eight. They live in Hopatcong, New Jersey, where Betty has been president of the local Mothers of Twins Club.

BETTY: My husband was ecstatic when he found out we were going to have twins.

RAMSAY: I remember I was in front of the house working. She came up the driveway and said, "Guess what. Better sit down. The X-ray showed two spines."

BETTY: It was funny, because during my first pregnancy, he had always said that I would have twins. It was like a premonition. When they were younger, we dressed them the same much more frequently than we do now. We were quite proud that they were twins; we wanted everybody to know. Now, I just feel that as they get older, they have to have their own identity. You get that kind of feedback from psychologists, doctors and everybody else.

They didn't know they were twins until they went to nursery school, because we never referred to them as "the twins." We always called them by their names. So they didn't know what a twin was. Then in nursery school, of course, the children began to mix them up. My girls get very indignant if someone calls them by the wrong name.

RAMSAY: Once, I played a trick on Betty when I was taking care of the babies. I switched them.

BETTY: I was out. I came home, fed them and put them back in their cribs. Then about an hour later, he said, "Did you see anything different?" They were only a couple of months old, and if you are not really looking, you don't see the differences. He was very much amused, because I used to say I knew how to tell them apart and he couldn't.

RAMSAY: I have trouble even now telling them apart, unless I see them smile.

BETTY: Amy has dimples and Jessica has two chipped front teeth, but if you don't see them a lot, it is very hard to pick up the differences. Even in identical twins, there is always some small difference, but if the person is not interested in seeing the differences, there is no way you can reach them. One funny thing with my girls—until about seven or eight months ago, Jessica was always good-natured, lovable, giving in to her sister. If Amy wanted to wear a particular dress, Jessica would let her. But about eight or nine months ago, Jessica made a complete about-face. Now she is the more difficult of the two. If I holler at them, she is the one who will become hysterical and Amy will just shrug and say, "Okay, Mom." For a couple of months it was really nerve-racking for me. I thought I knew the personality of my child. But basically, they are very similar in personality and they get along well, they really do. They have their differences, but they don't have nasty fights. I think it's just a natural thing, because even when they were younger, they would go back and forth. This week Amy would be more aggressive, and next week it would be Jessica's turn. This type of switching often happens with twins.

145

Donald & Louis Keith

Donald

Donald Keith is a retired Army lieutenant colonel. His twin, Louis Keith, is an obstetrician and gynecologist. Together they founded the Center for the Study of Multiple Gestation in Chicago, Illinois.

DONALD: Our parents gave us a lot of gifts—the gift of love, the gift of attention, the gift of a good home, the gift of culture, the gift of a good education—but the most important gift they gave to each of us was an individual sense of identity. We were separated in the third grade. My mother said we were being separated and that was the end of it. I guess she and the school counselors decided it would be smart and, from that day on, we never attended another class together in grammar school, high school or college even. We didn't even go to the same college.

LOUIS: The day we left for college, we walked out the door, and he turned to the right, I turned to the left. Only my father noticed this. He said, "Come back here, you must say goodbye to each other." We were seventeen.

DONALD: We weren't even friendly until we were twenty-eight, but we became friends in 1963 when I got married. We were competitors and each of us tried to pour the other into his mold. When we finally realized that couldn't be, we became friends. Then we began to collaborate and to communicate, and that's when we found out that we had ESP.

LOUIS: There's no question about it. My brother and I have it. He is the sender and I am the receiver. He can get me to call by putting out what he calls "vibrations," and I go to the phone. It's been going on for years.

DONALD: I'll think, "Louis, I wish you'd call me," and let my mind freewheel, and—ding-ding—the phone will ring. Louis will be there, saying, "Just felt like calling."

LOUIS: I'll be sitting doing nothing and I'll call
Donald, just like that. Our conversations never
begin, they never end, they only continue. The
phone will ring, he'll pick it up and say, "You
got my vibration," and then we go on. See, he
doesn't say, "Hello," and we don't say, "Goodbye," and so on. Why should we? It's a forty-
four-year conversation. But that's the only
thing. I've never felt when he was ill, he's never
felt when I was ill, I've never felt when he was
wounded in war. No, this is the only thing we
have—telephonic communication—when he
wants to talk to me.

DONALD: So far, it will only work up to seven
hundred miles, and if he's tired, I can't get
through. And if he's in the operating room,
there's no way for me to get through. Every bit
of his mental energy is on the patient.

LOUIS: The bond between us is greater than between most brothers and sisters. Perhaps the
essence of being a twin is that when you wake
up, even if you're not in the same city or house
or room, there is another part of you some-
place else.

DONALD: Both of our wives are exceptionally understanding and that's a key, because if the
spouses don't understand the twin relationship,
you can have a divorce on your hands. The
spouse may have a regular relationship with a
brother or sister, without all the telephone
calls, and they don't understand the connection
between twins. I know that if anything happens
to me and my wife, that, as sure as I am sitting
in this room, my brother will assume the obligation of educating my children. When I'm in
trouble, I know there is somebody there. I will
do things for Louis that I will not do for anybody else and he will do things for me that he
wouldn't do for anybody else. It's unspoken.
It's just there.

Louis

ON BEING TWINS

Most of us are not twins. Or are we? Look in the mirror. Is not your right half a duplicate of your left? Think about your heart, your lungs, and your kidneys. Is not the right half of each a duplicate of its left? In fact, the inclination to duplicate is in each of us. In some of us, however, this inclination is so powerful that we double ourselves entirely, producing a duplicate embryo, exact in each and every one of the 50,000 genes contained in each of our cells. We become identical twins—as alike as the right and left halves of our body.

Dr. Blair O. Rogers, the plastic surgeon who pioneered the transplantation of skin between individuals, believes that identical twins are essentially one and the same person, except for the thought processes of their brains and their personalities. He says, "Although separated in the womb, they share the successful transplantability of their skin, their kidneys, their corneas—everything. If we knew how to transplant nerve tissue successfully, it should be possible to transplant a portion of brain tissue from one twin to the other if it were necessary. Only with identicals could you theoretically do that."

The splitting which results in identical twins takes place after the father's germ cell (his sperm) has fertilized the mother's germ cell (her egg). The resulting zygote, the cell produced by the union of these two germ cells, multiplies by dividing in half. Hence, identical twins are technically referred to as "monozygotic" twins.

Contrary to popular belief, identical twins do not run in families. It is thought that there are no genes for the splitting of a fertilized egg, that this splitting is triggered by something other than genetic message. Dr. Gordon Allen, medical statistician at the National Institute of Mental Health, reports that every couple in each pregnancy has one chance in 270 of bearing identical twins; those odds are no different among couples in whose families there is a history of identical twinning.

THE BIOLOGY OF TWINNING

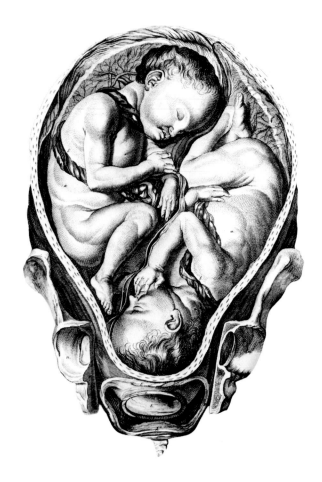

Twins in Utero.
Engraving by Josef von Morenheim, 1791.
Courtesy of the Rare Book Library,
New York Academy of Medicine.

Fraternal twins are another matter entirely. Polyovulation, the tendency of a woman to release more than one egg at a time, does seem to be genetically influenced. When two eggs are released into the Fallopian tubes simultaneously, both are available for fertilization, but by two different spermatozoa. The resulting children are technically referred to as "dizygotic" or "fraternal" twins and share a common prenatal environment as well as the same birth date. Of course, they can be either girl/girl, boy/boy or girl/boy.

Approximately one birth in 150 is of fraternal twins; thus most women have one chance in 150 with each pregnancy of bearing fraternal twins. Among women who have already borne one set of fraternal twins, however, this chance jumps to about one in forty, says Allen. And for a woman whose mother has had fraternal twins, the frequency is about one in ninety. A man as well as a woman can carry the gene for polyovulation, though, of course, the tendency will be manifested only in his female offspring, who may then polyovulate and bear fraternal twins.

It is speculated that there may be yet a third type of twin, sometimes referred to as "identical/fraternal." This type may be the result of duplication of the mother's egg prior to fertilization, and then fertilization by two different spermatozoa. The twins share their mother's contribution to their genetic blueprint, and owe their differences to their father.[2] Since it is the father's germ cell which determines the sex of the offspring, these twins may be of either sex. This may explain why some boy/girl twins are so similar in appearance.

In the case of monozygotic twins, if division of the fertilized egg takes place after the first ten days of development but before the thirteenth, the twins are often found to be mirror images.[3] While one may be left-handed, the other may be right-handed; hair whorls may go clockwise on one and counterclockwise on the other; a birthmark on the right side of one may be on the left side of the other; while one crosses arms left over right, the other may cross right over left. In the case of the Dionne identical quintuplets, it appears that Marie and Emilie were the last to separate because they were mirror images.

If the fetus divides after the thirteenth day, separation may be incomplete.[4] A physical linkage between the two may leave them joined at any part of the body, possibly sharing vital organs. The most famous of conjoined twins were Chang and Eng, nineteenth-century twins from Siam, joined by a band at the breastbone. They traveled with P. T. Barnum's circus as human curiosities and were famous here and abroad. It is with Chang and Eng that the term "Siamese twins" originated.

Triplets are the result of three eggs being released and fertilized (fraternals); two eggs being released, one of which splits after fertilization (two identicals and one fraternal); or one egg being released and fertilized, and then splitting into two identical zygotes, one of which then splits again (identicals).

The Dionne quintuplets, born in 1934, were originally one egg fertilized by one sperm. The resulting zygote split into two, both of which again split into two. Finally, one of the four resulting embryos split again, creating the fifth child.[5] The Dionnes are the only known identical quintuplets. Cecile, Yvonne, and Annette, now forty-six years old, live in Canada.

Natural curiosity, one would think, would cause even the most look-alike twins to want to know whether they are monozygotic or dizygotic. And if natural curiosity is not the driving force, sometimes the fight for survival is. For Darryl Wirick of Lake Placid, Florida, it was the survival of his brother Darren which served as the impetus.[6] Darren was born with a tiny kidney, insufficient to keep him alive. Tissue studies revealed that his body would reject a donation from either of his parents. Eight-year-old Darryl went before a judge to express his determination to donate a kidney to his brother. The fact that Darryl and Darren are monozygotic twins assured nearly 100 percent acceptance of the donation, as opposed to 85 percent acceptance from any other sibling, 60 percent from a parent or 50 percent from a nonrelative.[7] At last report, the donation was, indeed, accepted.

Where a determination of zygocity is necessary, a skin-graft test provides the needed information. The test involves the grafting of a small circle of skin from the inside forearm of one twin to that of the other. Such a graft will remain intact for more than thirty days only on monozygotic twins. If the skin sloughs off, the twins know they are dizygotic.[8]

The skin-graft test is highly accurate. It is also inconvenient, and used primarily when an organ transplant or treatment of a burn victim is at stake. For pure satisfaction of curiosity, twins may have their handprints and footprints analyzed for similarity of ridge patterns. Called "dermatoglyphics," this process is used by Dr. H. Warner Kloepfer, of Tulane University, who hypothesizes that if twins are identical genetically, they should have virtually identical prints.

Fraternal twins.
Jonathan and Jennifer Michaels.

Identical twins.
Noel and Holly Geremia.

Identical triplets.
Angella, Claudine and
Claudette Mawby.

Identical quintuplets.
Yvonne, Annette, Cecile, Emilie and Marie Dionne,
the only known identical quintuplets.

Fraternal quintuplets.
Abigail, Ted, Sarah, Gordon
and Amy Kienast.

TWINS IN OTHER CULTURES

Yoruba Ibeji Figures of Female Twins.
Nigeria, Africa. Collection of the Brooklyn Museum.

The Yoruba statues, *ibeji*, carved to represent twins who had "gone away," were always given mature adult features. They were regularly offered food, cleaned, dressed and adorned with cosmetics and jewelry.

Throughout history twins have been received with both pleasure and displeasure. Probably nowhere are twins more revered than among the Yoruba of western Nigeria. Yoruba mothers of twins practice weekly rituals of devotion honoring their twins by dancing and singing special lullabies publicly. Passersby acknowledge the importance of twins by offering money to the dancing mothers. Thus twins are associated with a rise in the family fortune.

Such loving attention was not always conferred on Yoruba twins. Anthropologists report that in earlier times twins were feared for their supernatural powers and ritually slaughtered (a practice not uncommon in primitive societies). According to the Yoruba, long ago when non-twin Yoruba children began to die mysterious deaths, terrified parents consulted an oracle, who commanded them to stop killing the twins at once. Instead, they were told to honor their twins in order to dissuade the spirits of the slaughtered twins from killing other children.

Even today, the Yorubas do not acknowledge death in twins. Yoruba twins do not die; they "go away," always leaving open the possibility that they might at any time return. Yoruba twins also have the power to cause the sickness or death of their parents and siblings, and have power over their mother's ability to bear more children. In addition, after they have "gone away," their power increases, due to their closer proximity to the spirit world. The Yoruba believe that if they provide special care for a twin who has "gone away," he or she may be attracted back and be reborn. Thus, during the time the mother is capable of childbearing, she confers devotional rites on a surrogate of the missing twin—a wooden statue, eight to eleven inches high, carved to specify the sex of the twin and the twin's family markings. Called an ibeji, the Yoruba word for twins, the statue allows the mother to give the same honors to both twins, though only one may be alive. Unequal treatment

Yoruba Women Dancing in the Marketplace with Ibeji Statues.
Courtesy of Dr. Robert F. Thompson.

Though their twins are no longer living, these Yoruba women continue to honor them by dancing and singing with wooden statues representing their deceased children.

could bring disaster, causing resentment and anger. The surrogate figure is periodically washed and dressed, and adorned with cosmetics and jewelry. It is kept on the twins' altar, built at the time of their birth.

As long as the twins are small enough to be carried, the mother straps them to her body with a side sash when she performs her ritual weekly dance. If one has "gone away," she carries the surviving child and tucks the wooden figure of the other in her sash. If both are gone, she carries an ibeji of each and continues to honor them with weekly dancing and singing.

To pacify twins, Yoruba mothers feed them a special food. One mother explained: "One eats beans to cool one's temper. So one serves beans to the twins to please them and to cool them down so they won't cause trouble. The beans are cooked with oil. Oil is to pacify trouble and so are beans. Therefore, oil and beans cool double trouble." [9]

Twins are special to many native American Indian tribes today. Their present attitudes are rooted in the legends that have long surrounded twins in their culture. They, along with the Yoruba, believed that twins may leave this world at will and that they came originally from heaven and returned there as they chose. The Mohave Indians believed that there were more twins in heaven than ever come to visit on earth. Those who did come, were here to sightsee, to visit, and to swim. [10]

The Yuman Indians of the Colorado River believed that because twins came from heaven they possessed rainmaking abilities. When drought threatened the crops, the twins in heaven picked up rocks and rolled them back and forth, causing thunder and finally rain. [11]

Many rituals evolved in these tribes to entice the twins not to leave the earth. Parents in several tribes set twins apart from the other children by dressing them alike in colors considered to be cloud colors—red, black and white. [12] Twins were

given equal gifts, for if one twin was favored, the other might become angry and return to heaven. Anthropologist George Devereaux observed the importance of these ancient traditions as recently as 1939, noting that in the Mohave tribe the relatives of newborn twins gathered treasured items, divided them into two equal piles and brought them to the twins as gifts. Often the Mohaves gave seeds stored for planting for the coming year—an extremely generous gesture in the light of their chronic poverty. All these gifts were intended to ensure that the twins stay with the tribe and bring good fortune to the people. [13]

Some peoples believed contact with animals who normally have multiple births might lead to the birth of twins. The Pueblos thought that eating bread baked by a deer hunter might result in the birth of twins. [14] Other foods also have been avoided by those who wished to prevent conception of twins. In France and England, women have traditionally refused to eat any double fruit or nut, double-yolked eggs, or bananas with split skins. [15] The Zulu of southeast Africa refused to eat two animals caught in the same trap. [16]

Among some African tribes, twins are so feared that young women are forbidden to listen to tales of them, lest they become susceptible to twin conception. [17] In the Niger delta, quarreling women curse each other by holding up two fingers, a gesture meaning "May you be the mother of twins." [18]

Clearly among nomadic tribes who must carry their children on their backs from place to place, and among agricultural people who must tend their children as they work in the fields, a double birth means an excessive burden for the mother. This might explain why in the past twins were considered a curse and were immediately put to death. Today, infanticide is universally a criminal offense, [19] and twins are spared that fate. It is doubtful, however, that they will quickly lose their reputation for supernatural power. After all, why are there two where there is usually only one?

THE PSYCHOLOGY OF TWINS

Do identical twins have identical personalities? It was the British scientist Sir Francis Galton who, just over a century ago, first proposed that twins would be naturally ideal for the study of genetic vs. environmental influences on behavior, or "nature vs. nurture." He thus developed gemellology, the study of twins. A century later, at the 1977 International Congress on Twin Studies, nearly a hundred papers were presented covering such topics as sexual attitudes among twins, depression, socioeconomic status, birth defects, heart disease, albinism and the effects of vitamin C on colds.

Sweden has collected information on more than 23,000 pairs of twins. More than 15,000 twins in Rome receive free medical care for life through Dr. Luigi Gedda's Institut di Gemellogia. They must be seen together for all examinations. In the United States, a national registry is maintained of 16,000 sets of twins in which both have served in the armed forces. In California, the Kaiser-Permanente medical group stores information on 8,000 sets of twins. And throughout the country, groups of mothers of twins cooperate by filling out questionnaires for researchers on hundreds of projects. Thus twins throughout the world are being viewed as human "laboratories" in which genes are examined via the behaviors they create. Data on these studies on twins reared together are still being processed and analyzed, and definitive conclusions on the heredity vs. environment issue have yet to be achieved.

Identical twins reared apart are providing scientists with the opportunity to view the effects of the same genetic material subjected to different environments, since similarities may be ascribed to heredity.

Dr. Thomas J. Bouchard, Jr., of the University of Minnesota, is testing twins reared apart for such personality traits as dominance, self-acceptance, responsibility, tolerance and flexibility. While his data-gathering is in preliminary stages, he says there is a "strong suggestion that twins reared apart may be more similar than if they had been reared together." This view has also been presented by the French researcher Rene Zazzo, who says, "Genetic factors appear to play a very significant role when the twins live apart, but almost completely disappear when the twins live together." [20] Bouchard says there is a "natural propensity to develop a certain way, which is given more rein when twins are reared apart than when they are together. They seem to react off each other," he explains. Zazzo calls this reaction "the couple effect." Suggesting that the term "environment" is too closely associated with society and culture, Zazzo reminds us that each twin's environment includes his co-twin. "Dominance," he notes, "may result from higher birthweight or better physical conditions, or even from having been designated and then treated as the elder twin, whatever the criteria the parents follow in so doing. It is indeed amusing," he adds, "to see that fifty percent of the parents consider as elder the first born, and fifty percent the second born. What is important, however, is to be considered as such. The 'we,' " he points out, "is anterior to the 'I' and determines it." In other words, in the absence of a follower, there can be no leader.

In addition to scientific data, Dr. Bouchard's studies have uncovered information which borders on the supernatural. Among the pairs being studied are the "Jim Twins." Placed for adoption immediately upon birth, these twins were separated at the age of four weeks when one was adopted by the Ernest Springers and the other by the Jess Lewises. Unknown to each other, both couples named their sons James. At the age of thirty-nine, Jim Lewis fulfilled an urge to go to court to find his brother, and a reunion followed. "I looked into his eyes and saw a reflection of myself," said Springer, who had been told his twin brother had died at birth. "I wanted to scream or cry, but all I could do was laugh."

Since their reunion, Springer and Lewis have learned that:

Both are divorced from women named Linda and married to women named Betty.

Springer named his first son James Allan and Lewis named his first son James Alan.

Each has an adopted brother named Larry.

Each named a pet dog Toy.

Each had law-enforcement training and had been a part-time deputy sheriff in Ohio.

Both did mechanical drawing, block lettering and carpentry.

Both did well in math and poorly in spelling.

Each drove a Chevrolet from Ohio to the same vacation stop—a three-block-long beach area in Florida.

Both are six feet tall and weigh 180 pounds.

Both gained ten pounds at the same point in adulthood.

Both suffer from tension headaches. In each case, the headache syndrome began at age eighteen. The men use nearly identical language to describe it.

Springer and Lewis were raised in the same country and by nuclear families.

Another set of identical twins reunited through participation in the Minnesota project does not share even these factors. Oskar Stohr and Jack Yufe, separated at six months and reunited at age forty-seven, were reared in entirely different cultures. Stohr was raised as a Catholic in Nazi Germany by women—his mother and grandmother. Yufe was raised by his Jewish father, joined an Israeli kibbutz when he was seventeen, and later served in Israel's Navy. They had different religions, spoke different languages, and were exposed to different styles of child-rearing. Yet

Bouchard said he was struck by the similarities in their behavior. Their style of walking, sitting and eating, their rate of speech, their temperament and the types of questions they ask are all similar. Both like spicy foods, fall asleep after eating and are absent-minded. Both store rubber bands on their wrists, read magazines back to front, flush the toilet before and after using, and like to startle strangers by sneezing loudly in otherwise quiet places. Both wore double-pocketed blue leisure suits with epaulets to their first meeting. Both have clipped mustaches and large, rectangular eyeglass frames. Both are married and have two children.

Ruth Johnson and Allison Erb were reunited after twenty-six years of separation. Each began the search for the other after having watched the same talk show on television. Both are hairdressers and wear their hair in the same style. Both have two children, one each named Kristen. When they met, Mrs. Erb said, "It was like looking in a mirror. I couldn't say anything."

Among other twins under study by Bouchard are a man with children named Andrew Richard and Catherine Louise, and his twin brother who has children named Richard Andrew and Karen Louise. (Karen had been chosen over the parents' preferred Katherine in order to honor a particular aunt.) One man had been told for years that someone in the next town looked exactly like him. Shortly after he joined the Navy, he decided to check the information out. He visited the town and wandered around until someone greeted him by a name not his own. "That's not who I am," he said, "but could you tell me where he lives?" He knocked on the door of his twin's home, startling the woman who answered. Her adopted son had just joined the Navy and she was surprised to see him at home.

TWIN BONDING

Donald M. Keith and Dr. Louis Keith, the identical twins discussed earlier, are co-directors of the Center for the Study of Multiple Gestation. Donald says, "Twins don't compete with each other. They compete together against others." He is speaking of a bond with which identical twins are familiar. "The bond is a special thread between twins, a psychological thread. It's an electrical window in the mind of identical twins, because they are from the same egg and the same sperm." This bond may manifest itself as a similar response to stimuli, which may also simply be the result of years of sharing, or it may seem to result in a heightened sense of telepathy or extrasensory perception.

Some twins report a mysterious phenomenon of sympathetic pain. Donald Keith recalls one woman's account of shared pain between her two-and-a-half-year-old granddaughters. She was caring for one of the twins while the other was in the hospital for eye surgery. At the moment of the surgeon's incision, the child at home, who knew nothing of the surgery, screamed out in pain, clutching her eye. Professional basketball player Faye Young fainted during the setting of her broken finger. In a high school gym twenty miles away, her twin sister Kaye fainted simultaneously. Bruce Ellis described (page 112) the occasion of the rupturing of his appendix. Jeff spent the day in the school infirmary with severe stomach cramps. "We always take these coincidences for granted," says Bruce.

Eerily, the twin bond has been reported among people whose twin died before or shortly after birth. One physician says he always felt oddly attuned to twins, to the point of dreaming that he was a twin. Upon questioning his mother, he learned that a mass of tissue had been born with him. He believes the mass was the lost twin who has haunted his dreams.

The medical phenomenon of only one twin surviving past birth has been dubbed, "the vanishing twin." [21] Scientists have found that, on occasion, ultrasonic examination accurately diagnoses a twin pregnancy, and then only one infant develops and is born, the other having been absorbed into the body. The infant born is considered a surviving twin.

Other survivor twins lose their partners shortly after birth. Stephanie Feil, director of the Montessori Children's House of Manhattan, reports that her twin sister died of complications following birth. "Even though I didn't know my sister," she says, "I feel that I did. I've always thought of myself as a twin; I feel a rapport with other twins."

In fact, fewer than 60 percent of twins are carried a full nine months before being born. This high incidence of premature births results in an equally high rate of infant mortality. Mortality during the first month of life is five times higher among twins than among singletons.[22] "Every time you see cute little twins in a double stroller, you don't think of them as survivors," says Donald Keith. "But they are."

Donald Keith has considerable concern for twins who find themselves alone later in life. "I'm afraid we're going to see some severe psychological problems with the generation of twins now in their fifties, sixties and seventies as they begin to lose their partners. In their early years," he explains, "it was the vogue to 'unit-raise'; therefore they cannot function individually. If a person loses his will to live because his twin dies, this is a doubly tragic situation." In fact, it is not unheard of that after the death of one twin, the other will also cease to live, with no apparent cause of death. In addition to recommending that twin survivors seek consolation from other twins and psychological assistance through therapy, Keith stresses that twins

should be raised as individuals. "They can't be the 'cute little twins' forever," he says. "They should be prepared for this."

Louis Keith says he and his brother recognized the need for separation by the time they were ten or twelve. "Some of the other twins in the school we went to were psychological cripples. When one went to the john, the other went with him. Certain things in life, you want to do alone." One mother overheard her twins saying, "Let's pretend we're brothers." When she told them they were brothers, they responded, "No, we're not. We're twins." Similarly, some twins report they fear others will not recognize them if they are not together. Clearly, it is the twin status which is invisible when each is alone. "They must learn," says Donald Keith, "that that person over there is not me. It's not a body divided by two; it's two bodies."

Twin psychologists Judy Hagedorn and Janet Kizziar say that twins run the risk of developing the misconception during their youth that simply being twins is enough to assure success in life. "Since twins usually receive esteem, attention, identity and even popularity simply because they are twins," they say, "many probably feel little incentive to work for what they attain. They are likely to form an expectation of high esteem merely by making themselves noticeable. When they reach maturity, often identical twins have not developed motivation to excel or achieve." Hagedorn and Kizziar stress the need for the development of individuality and personal worth and importance. "Throughout life," they say, "what twins receive and what they achieve will not be identical."

One of the pitfalls of choosing similar occupations, say Hagedorn and Kizziar, is the inevitability of comparison, a process through which, they say, "one twin *always* suffers." Among the twins with whom they have worked, they have heard reports of such comments as, "You're a good hairdresser, but your twin is fantastic;" "Your twin only charged me ten dollars to do my plumbing. You did the same work and asked for fifteen dollars;" and "Your twin types sixty words per minute and is neat. You're so sloppy, I wouldn't keep you as my secretary, except that I'd hate to lose your sister."

Fortunately many sets of twins are able to deal with the threat of such comparison, and are able to follow their natural inclinations, however similar they may be. Hagedorn and Kizziar, for instance, enjoy being co-authors, sharing their thoughts and plans, stimulating their thinking through debate. "We tend to be each other's sternest critic, but we also enjoy being our twin's best friend and confidante," they say.

A perusal of the interviews of twins in this book reveals many examples of successful career choice. Christopher and David Alden produced puppet shows as young children. Today they are theatrical directors, working on separate operas, but sharing an interest in each other's work. Tim and Tom Gullikson never had to search for a tennis partner; the other was always there. Today they are top-ranked on the worldwide tennis circuit. Faye and Kaye Young began passing a basketball between them when they were in junior high school. Today they play professionally with the New York Stars. Charles and Wilmer Frederick live in separate homes on the same successful dairy farm in New Hope, Pennsylvania. Jeff and Bruce Ellis are doubly efficient at running a catering company.

For these individuals, being a twin has enhanced their career choices. As Donald Keith said, twins compete together against the rest of the world. They are their own best fans.

Ramsay and Betty Reid
with Ramsay, Jr., Amy and
Jessica and Jennifer.

ON HAVING TWINS

Psychologist Jane Hirschman-Levy was in the tenth week of her pregnancy when she learned that she was carrying twins. With so much time for preparation, she and her husband, Richard, read everything available and attended special classes on the care of twins. "Suddenly, boom, they were here," Jane recalls. "Nobody could have told me what it was going to be like—the work. They were all-consuming. There wasn't a moment to stop and think. You don't have that kind of time anymore. With one child, you figure there are two of you and you have a little bit of reserve energy. With two, the reserve is used up immediately. There is always a baby needing something. We had a lot of time to prepare, and I don't know how women do it who don't have that time, but we were never prepared. When they came, I was so overwhelmed, the breath was taken out of me. But I'm lucky because Richard is fabulous. He does as much as I do."

"Twins are one of the things you get in life without choosing," said Ruth Michaels, mother of Jennifer and Jonathan. "I never thought about twins until they were born. My delivery was six weeks early. When I saw these two red wrinkly raisins, I couldn't believe it! I was absolutely flying high. My husband's way of telling people was, 'Guess what. We just had a girl.' After they'd react, he'd say, 'And then we had a boy.'"

The shock of learning that there are two is often followed by the agony of waiting to handle them, since premature babies must remain in incubators for some time after birth. "They were perfect, but tiny," recalls Ruth Michaels. "New York State has a law that you can't bring your babies home until they weigh five pounds. Talk about postpartum blues. They were carried off to another hospital labeled Baby A and Baby B, and I was only allowed to visit for one hour on Sundays and Wednesdays. It was three weeks before I first held my son and daughter."

When Jennifer and Jonathan were ready to be taken home, Ruth Michaels was given an hour of training in the care of twins. "They showed me how to wrap the kimonos around three times to get them to fit, because the babies were so little." The hour of training cannot prepare parents for the demands of twin infants. For one thing, tiny babies run out of food quickly and consequently require extra-frequent feedings. "It's overwhelming," says Ruth, "and emotionally draining. The babies had different formulas. On the left-hand side of the refrigerator was one formula, and on the right side was the other. I had charts taped to the wall. That's how I discovered I'd fed the same baby twice in a row one day. It took me an hour just to get them ready to go out. And the laundry was overwhelming."

So special are the problems of raising twins that many mothers gather regularly to share information and lend encouragement to each other. Mothers of Twins Clubs exist in most states. Says Donald Keith, "To any woman carrying twins, I say immediately, get to a Mothers of Twins Club. They know what it's like."

"The biggest thing we give to a new mom," says Betty Reid of the New Jersey Mothers of Twins Clubs, "is a sympathetic ear and to say, 'You will live through it. The kids will sleep through the night.' We've all cried on the phone, saying, 'They won't stop crying,' etcetera, but just to be able to talk to somebody who you know has gone through the same problem can help. Each age has a different problem. For the new moms, it is just the sheer physical work involved in taking care of two. We tell the mothers, 'Your babies are more important than your housework. When you have tiny twins, you'll find the dust is going to be there forever. Let that go. Take care of your babies and take care of yourself. You and the babies are more important than any housework.' It also helps to have a husband who is helpful. And another thing is to have time for your husband. No matter how busy you are, it is important to get a baby-sitter and get out by yourselves. Go have a cup of coffee in a diner, anything, just to be with each other. Because if you lose that, then there goes the family, and it can be very trying to have twins alone."

ADVICE ON REARING TWINS

The following suggestions were made in a book called *The Care of Twin Children* published by the Center for the Study of Multiple Gestation.[23]

The goal of raising twins is to bring each of them to mature adulthood, capable of making independent decisions that affect their lives, such as choice of career, job, or marriage partner. Without learning the necessary skills during their formative years for making their own choices, they become emotionally incapable of functioning independently.

● The home environment and parents' attitudes tend to mold the children's personalities to a great extent. If the twins are thought of and treated as a unit, they will think of themselves as only halves of a whole and act accordingly. If "twinny" behavior is allowed and thought to be cute and acceptable, it will impede both children in recognizing their own uniqueness and separateness. Confusion of identity by relatives, teachers, and others may only compound the problem.

● There are many ways to foster individuality without destroying the special bond of twinship.

● If you have problems telling your babies apart when you bring them home from the hospital, you can leave their name bands on, put nail polish on one baby's toenail, or use different colored diaper pins or clothing on each baby. Among sets of identical twins, one child always has a rounder or fuller face, which should help you and others tell the babies apart.

● Consider following the practice of many parents who use unlike-sounding names for their twins, especially in the case of identicals or look-alike fraternals.

● Never call your children "Twinny" or even refer to them as "the twins"; ask others to avoid this also. Call both children by their names more frequently than normal to reinforce their individuality in their own minds.

● Give each child some special time alone with you.

● Take pictures of your children separately as well as together.

● Give both space for their own belongings, and, if conditions allow, give them separate rooms.

● Use different colors in look-alike clothing to establish easy, quick identification.

● Joining a play group, babysitting co-op, or nursery school is a good way to expose your pre-schoolers to other children on a regular basis.

● Discuss your ideas about individuality with the teachers at the beginning of school. They can do much to help the twins separate by placing them in different activity groups and encouraging each child to pursue his own special interests.

● Allow children to begin to make choices at an early age, two or three years, in such things as clothes, toys, or other minor areas of their daily routine.

● Encourage different interests in each child's life so the children will be called on to make independent decisions affecting them personally. Allow each child to choose his own personal experiences; for example, one may want to play the violin, the other to take judo lessons.

● Assign each child different chores.

● Never compare the children's performances. With everyone else comparing them, one twin may begin to measure himself against the other, feeling he lacks some quality the other supposedly possesses. Unless they realize their own individuality, know they are special persons in their own right, then one or both children may lose confidence in themselves and their abilities. The result may be behavioral or school-related problems, or intense competition to make up for imagined deficiencies.

● Although the twins may have been apart for short periods and played with different children, separation in school gives each child completely different environments and experiences. For the first time, each is accepted by teachers and classmates as a single person rather than as "the twins." Although they may miss each other, most twins adjust well to separation, especially if individuality has been stressed. The realization that they can function independently of each other brings a special feeling of pride and accomplishment.

TELLING TWINS APART

"It was really hard to tell them apart," says Frances Whiteman. "When Rochelle and Michelle were born twelve years ago, I kept a name tag on their wrists for about a month." The Whitemans are from Lodge Grass, Montana, and are native Americans, members of the Crow tribe. Recently, at the age of twelve the girls received their ceremonial names which it is believed will help them in life. Rochelle is called Aasuuaxiasaalakus, meaning "having a home that always welcomes anybody and everybody." Michelle's name in the Crow language is Apaalitchish, "going in good health and leading a good life."

"As the girls grew I figured out that the shape of their faces is different. Rochelle has a wider forehead and a wider, rounder cheek. Michelle has a narrower forehead and a longer face than her sister. Later on I tied different color ribbons on their braids. Rochelle likes red or orange; Michelle prefers blue or green. As we grew together I learned Michelle is always in a good mood and cheerful, and Rochelle is more moody. People do notice this and make comments. I don't think that the child should be told that he or she is moody or bad. I have had this experience and it is hard to deal with. I would always answer 'They both have their times of being moody and they both have their times of being cheerful.'"

"The girls love to dance and sing. They know the lullabies of our people, and the Round Dance song, and the Warrior Dance song.

"They do fight a lot but they are very close. They are really very protective of each other. They have special communication with each other, a language with words that are a mixture of Crow and English. They say, 'Dii wuulibuk you! (I don't like you) or Come huuchwa! (Come here).' When I have to ask what the words mean, they tell me.

"In our culture twins are considered a special gift."

Rochelle and Michelle Whiteman, Native American twins of the Crow Tribe; Rochelle (on the left) has a narrower face and wider cheeks.

Mary & Peggy Roblee

THE ROBLEE TWINSHIP

Mary and I are always amazed that people are so curious about us. We still do look absurdly alike, especially after we have been together a few days. We are curious about twins too, and always feel a special bond toward other identical twins. A kind of conspiracy of understanding.

Obviously, when I am looking at my sister, I see only her. I cannot see myself, so do not see the twin image that others observe. That is, unless we look into the mirror together, and then we are struck with amusement at the resemblance, and understand why we are such a subject for amusement and curiosity by others.

Newly born we were indecipherable. Mary was wrapped with a blue ribbon, I with a pink. They have been our colors ever since. Family reports are that we were always both independent and interdependent and consequently did not need the attention of others.

We spoke our own language as babies, according to our mother, which no one else could understand. We still speak our own language together—a combination of English, French and Spanish, plus many allusions that leave our poor husbands totally perplexed and sometimes annoyed.

We had an imaginary playmate named Buga, with his house, the Buga Box—a white wicker toy chest where he was either taken out or put away at whim. He was our constant companion until we were about five. It was definitely a he and not a she, though I have no idea of what he looked like, even though we both remember him very well, even to the last day when we said goodbye to him and put him back into his box forever.

We always went to the same schools—eighteen of them in various states and countries, and could not have survived all those changes without each other.

Genetically we are a split egg—the same genes— so there is a ninety percent correlation in identical twins. We have the same I.Q. and always got the same marks and excelled in the same subjects of history and English and music and art history, and failed math. We dressed alike until we were nineteen, and then switched our clothes around. We still often buy the same dress in different colors, as the same things are becoming to both of us and we have the same taste.

When we separated, it was difficult to find a solo direction, and I missed the support and company of my sister. I felt shy and insecure, but eventually was able to make my own directions. I feel my sister has always been the more agressive and adventurous of the two of us—less shy and sensitive. I was always proud of her success or fame and I think she has been of mine. Sometimes we shone together, sometimes separately—stars in the same galaxy. If there was ever a struggle over a man, we just backed off. We'd prefer not to have the man than to have the struggle.

We have always gotten along perfectly well together. The only barrier has been husbands who are resentful of the time we spend together, who insist on creating tension for more attention. Children have been understanding and not demanding, though I'm sure there have been times when they resented the close twin relationship. I have children—my sister does not. We often tried to fool my children as babies, but they always knew. Perhaps they are the only ones, as our mother and our husbands have mistaken us more than once.

I think that most people who marry twins really don't know what they're in for. And consequently, there is a good deal of resentment on the part of the spouse toward the twin's twin. Jealousy of the close relationship that a split egg implies. I can understand it but do not enjoy the rejection that it can generate. On the other hand, I think that my husband genuinely enjoys the "pasha" role of having two for company instead of one.

When we are together, we tend to exclude others—our husbands and children and others. The twin language seems to dominate the others and we never run out of conversation, even though some of it is often repeated. Also, we laugh a good deal together and have our own jokes and obscure allusions and language. I do feel there is a cosmic relation between twins. This probably makes relationships with others more remote, more difficult. Often I have dreams that predict an event described in a crossing letter. As we live so often on opposite continents, we feel there definitely is a psychic telepathy between us. When one is ill or emotionally upset, the other worries, frets and wonders about the other. Malaise.

We vacation together whenever possible. We have a joint bank account and we like the same things—music, art, theater, films, museums, architecture, history. We live with each other very easily, but I do not suppose we are too easy for others—too mercurial. We like other twins and have a kind of conspiracy friendship with them. Identical twins, that is.

Perhaps twins understand love better than most and make great lovers when they fall under the spell of Eros. I do feel to be a twin is to have reached a certain evolvement in the scale of incarnation—a kind of reward for other lives given to a privileged few.

—Peggy Roblee Donovan

My twin sister is the one person I cannot imagine the world without. The best gift for anyone in life is to be a twin. Being an identical twin means never to know alienation, disapproval or rejection, because one's twin is always there, somewhere in the universe, the mirror self, radiating this shared acceptance, no matter what the circumstances, whether happy or unhappy.

From childhood, we clung together, having our own language and an imaginary playmate named "Buga" until we started school. As alike as two drops of water, we were dressed alike, but Peggy wore a touch of pink, and I, a touch of blue, so others could tell us apart. We always gave the best to each other or shared everything completely, whether a toy or a sweet as children, or clothes or jewels or money as adults. We have always lived in an aura of mutual trust and admiration with the absolute knowledge that no obstacles of Andes, Rockies or ocean seas could prevent one or the other from coming to the rescue in case of danger—whether physical, mental, emotional, financial or spiritual. No question as to whose side you're on: the twin is the winner, the perfect one, the light, the center of the universe.

Our emotional lives have not been thwarted by our own closeness, in that we both married and have lived in different countries during our adult life. A year never passed, however, that we were not together at some time, for holidays and visits back and forth. We have always had a flourishing correspondence with weekly letters flying across the Atlantic and telephone calls constantly when in different cities and countries. Our letters cross with identical paragraphs and fantasies and plans and options, some of which we realize.

Instinctively, we choose completely different types of men. I think this is a defense mechanism, a subconscious choice, as the conflict of competition in the sexual arena could be disastrous to our own relationship. Peggy veers toward the heros: tall, blond, Anglo-Saxons; whereas I prefer the stars: dark, lithe Latins. Our husbands are completely different.

I think it must be difficult for a man to be married to an identical twin, because twins are apt to go off into their own orbit, a kind of closed-circuit

Peggy Roblee Donovan
and Mary Roblee Henry.

communication that excludes others. On the other hand, it is also very nice. Twins are used to sharing, to giving each other the best, always to refer to the couple as "we," as they do to themselves. It works best when both twins are with one husband, making him feel rather a "pasha"—laughing at his jokes, listening to his political opinions, arranging a party for him, shining in front of his friends. When both couples are together, the men seem to become competitive and even to side against us. Subconsciously, I feel, they resent our impenetrable closeness, to the point of creating situations where my twin sister and I are forced to reject each other in favor of them—the territorial imperative, like a stallion marking his ground. It makes us both furious to realize that we have succumbed to this form of emotional blackmail.

She is a good brake for me. More impetuous, adventurous to the point of foolishness, I am fickle, feckless and faithless. If I am too adventurous and impulsive, she shows the opposite trait of good sense and caution. I encourage her to take chances and throw caution to the winds.

My work has to come first, but on all vacations I manage to spend some time with her and she with me. We have an irrepressible urge to be together after a few months apart and dash across borders or oceans to be together—like Castor and Pollux galloping through the skies. Septembers, we desert our husbands and spend a month in Paris, indulging our passion for music and books. We like the same foods—artichokes, avocados, asparagus, fish and fowl, very little red meat and no sweets, but cheeses and fruits and French wines. We always change at night into caftans or kurtas or gossamer pajamas. We love to dress up, to change identity. We are terribly vain and look at each other like looking in a mirror. We still wear our hair almost alike.

We toy with the idea of building the ideal house just for the two of us with a wing for each and a living room-dining room between. The perfect pool. The perfect colors. Perfection as we see it— American convenience, French charm.

The only moments of anger I know are caused by her sins of omission, refusing to confide when I might have been of help to her. Twins are always trying to spare each other the slings and arrows of life. I once had an operation in New York and did not tell my sister, sparing her a trip across the Atlantic to be with me, and she was furious.

I am a split egg, a half-person who must share each gene with another. That gives an understanding between humans that few experience. Only those involved in a cosmic love affair reach the same intersensitivity or communication. Perhaps twins make great lovers because they are born with that cosmic sense—mind lovers that lead to body lovers. There is a mysterious pagan element of twinship that seems to make all twins feel lucky to be twins and sorry for those who are not. Are we all like this in our smug approval, this special mirror image of superior beings, blessed by birth?

I cannot remember not feeling like a twin. It seems the most natural thing in the world. Plays and operas of mistaken identity I find normal. I once walked into a dressing room and faced a full-length mirror and exclaimed, "Oh, Peggy, I didn't know you were in here too." A twinship joke.

Above all, we adore each other and love being together. The agony would be to be in the world without her. If we must die, and we all must, I would like to die first.

—Mary Roblee Henry

Kathryn and Frances,
age six months.

ALL ABOUT US

FRANCES: We were born September 22, 1919, and were named Frances and Kathryn for our parents, Frank and Katherine McLaughlin. I was born first and Kathryn second; we arrived two months ahead of schedule on the day our parents were packed to move to their new home. Together we weighed less than eight pounds; we were snugly wrapped and placed near a warm oven and Father telephoned his friends to announce, "A flock of girls just arrived at our house." At age two Kathryn changed her name to Fuffy. First memories seem to be of a toy cupboard with beautiful doors in the playroom and the three imaginary friends we shared: Kayo, Maja and Afteryune. This was in New York City.

Four years later we moved to Wallingford, Connecticut, and started our schooling there. We lived in a big, cool dark green house trimmed in white with a large porch and grass all around. The fire chief and the police chief with their families lived next door. Directly across the street a few doors down to the right we found to our delight Betty and Lenore Moerschelle, twins who were a year younger than ourselves. They roamed the neighborhood taking the neighbors' milk from the steps, upsetting garbage pails and messing up the mail. When it rained they waded in the puddles wearing their Aunt Bessie's corsets and high-heeled shoes. (They went to Bennington College, became actresses, and later we were reunited and laughed together when they portrayed the twin daughters of Harriet Beecher Stowe on Broadway in a play starring Helen Hayes.) Betty and Lenore were allowed to chew tar from the roadway when it melted in the summer and to eat the pieces of ice that Mr. Mellor, the iceman, handed out. None of these things were permitted in our house.

When we were nine, twin girls, Janet and Joyce Stein, were born to the family who lived immediately to our left. We saw nothing unusual about one more set of twins. They became our new favorites; we dressed them, fed them, and wheeled them around the neighborhood. I felt a twinge of guilt when Joyce, who was my charge, turned out to be left-handed like me. I was convinced that somehow I had caused it.

With twins Betty and
Lenore Moerschelle.

With twins Janet and
Joyce Stein.

At Lake Compounce.

169

At the World's Fair, 1939.

KATHRYN: Frances and I did everything together. We adored my aunt's Kodak camera and begged to use it. She always said "Yes!" Twice a week we went to Wilkinson's movie theater; on Saturdays the matinee tickets were fifteen cents. We drew fashion drawings of sleek women with blowing scarves traveling with interesting men on cruise ships, dancing or sunning on the deck. We kept massive scrapbooks of our favorite film stars and acted out Saturday morning plays of our own. We shared one bicycle as the Andrettis did. The camera, not the bicycle, was our first love, however, and that was easier to share.

When my sister and I graduated from high school as class valedictorian and salutatorian our photograph was on the front page of the *New Haven Register*. That fall we entered the Art School of Pratt Institute in Brooklyn, equipped with one new Rolleicord camera ready to conquer the world. Here we are posing for our photography professor, Walter Civardi, during a field trip to the 1939 World's Fair. I am on the right. Our fashion look was strictly Peck & Peck: matching covert cloth coats, pork-pie hats and ankle socks. Photography was our favorite course and we spent hours in the darkroom. This was the year we decided we would become photographers. There was lots of good fun. Friends were always introducing us to men twins. We dated John and Bob Lawson, Yale '40, and caused riotous confusion when we four appeared at the Yale Prom that year. As seniors we each competed in *Vogue*'s Prix de Paris contest and were two of the five winners. This led to Frances's job as a photographer for *Vogue* magazine in 1943, where, by coincidence, I had landed a job as assistant to Toni Frissell, one of *Vogue*'s star photographers of the day. Having dressed alike during our school years we now chose to give up the twin look.

Double-image portrait
of Frances.

Studio photograph.
(Left to right) Fernand Fonssagrive.
James Abbe, Leslie Gill;
(foreground) Frances and Kathryn.

On the beach at Montauk, L.I.

Mrs. A. Willard Mellor with her twin daughters,
Alison and Susan

Mrs. Mellor, a tall, beautiful young woman who occasionally does modelling
for this magazine, has a chiselled profile, and melting brown eyes
which both her daughters, fortunately, inherit. Otherwise, they're quite different:
Alison (left) is blonder, calmer, more thoughtful; Susan (right) is darker,
faster-moving, "always running around." They're three and a half, and have been
dressing themselves since they were sixteen months old. With their parents
and a baby brother, Charles, known as C. J., they live in Locust Valley, where,
according to a friend, Mrs. Mellor "always underdresses—and does it very well."
With Mr. and Mrs. Hay (see page 145), the Mellors are involved in an amateur theatrical
company that has put on several plays for the benefit of local charities.

FRANCES MCLAUGHLIN

143

Without really planning it, in our twenties each of us married famous photographers. In 1946 I was married to James Abbe; in 1948 Frances married Leslie Gill. With four photographers in the family there were inevitably dozens of photographs. These are our favorites: the first taken by Jimmy on the beach at our summer home in Montauk, Long Island. I'm on the right; we are wearing bathing suits inspired by the latest Hawaiian designs. The other photograph is by Frances's husband, Leslie. With his meticulous touch he created his own interpretation of twins, combining two negatives of Frances in this one image. Designed perhaps to fool our friends?

FRANCES: At this point our marriages and our careers took us in quite different directions. The Abbes with their four children, a dog and a cat had moved to a Long Island farmhouse. Leslie and I lived busy, wonderful years in New York. As a photographer for *Vogue* and *Glamour,* I found the assignments exciting and demanding. Art director Alexander Liberman was an inspiration to his photographers. He sensed what was new before it quite materialized and created electricity in the air. These were fine years; a happy marriage, travel, new people, and an exchange of ideas. In 1957 I photographed a portfolio for *Vogue,* a feature on six families who lived near each other in Long Island who all had twin children. Often there were twin mix-ups such as the time a stranger threw his arms around Kathryn in Paris. It was a shocker whenever it happened. Often the

With our children.

(Left to right) Eli, Lucinda, and Tom Abbe; Frances and Leslie Gill and Kathryn Abbe, (foreground) the collie, Randy. Photographed by James Abbe, Jr., 1958.

person refused to believe that a twin existed.

Leslie Gill died suddenly in 1958 and we all pulled together to recover from this terrible tragedy. That summer Jimmy Abbe photographed us with the children. I am holding my daughter, Leslie; Eli Abbe is in the foreground; Tom and Lucinda are in the back with their mother Kathryn. Leslie became the special pet of her Abbe cousins and all of us spent happy times together. During these years, Kathryn and I continued our separate careers but shared our children and leisure hours whenever we could. She often arranged country locations for my photographs, and I provided studio facilities in New York when she needed them.

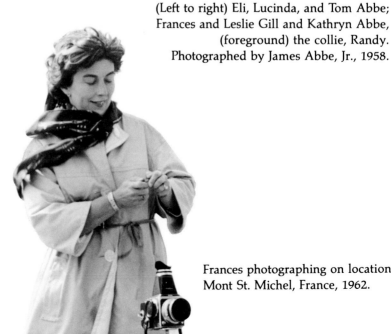

Frances photographing on location. Mont St. Michel, France, 1962.

The Kienast quints as new borns for *Good Housekeeping,* 1970. Photographed by Kathryn.

Better Homes and Gardens cover of the Kenny twins, 1973. Photographed by Kathryn.

KATHRYN: While Frances's photography took her on assignments around the world, I expanded my photography in different directions, photographing celebrities with their families, photographing my children for magazine illustrations. The world came to my doorstep. Among the many covers that each of us made for our magazines there were these two, of course, of twins. Frances's January 1964 cover for *Glamour* features the Gates twins. Whenever young beauties like the Gates sisters arrived in New York there was a scramble to be the first to photograph them. This time *Glamour* won with this cover layout by art director Miki Denhof.

One day in Montauk I spotted two four-year-olds playing in a telephone booth. They were the Kenny twins, full of fun, lively, with the brightest blue eyes. I whisked them off to the beach where they ran and leaped in the waves while I photographed. As we were finishing up the boys wrapped themselves in a towel. As I have seen so often with other twins, the Kennys moved naturally in tandem. The result—this 1973 summer cover for *Better Homes and Gardens.*

My all-time favorite assignment came from *Good Housekeeping* magazine when they asked me to be the exclusive photographer of the Kienast quintuplets. The babies were still in incubators when I first photographed them at Presbyterian Hospital in New York City. The problems involved in catching all five children in one photograph presented a real challenge. So I gathered my team. First, Frances helped out, together with my assistant. Later, when the five were toddlers and ran in all directions, I added to my crew my daughter, Lucinda, and my niece, Leslie, to work with the quints. Eventually we all were so close to the Kienasts that we came to think of them as our own and the Kienasts came to think of us as part of their family.

Documenting them year after year led us to many new thoughts about ourselves as twins and the specialness about being twins that we had come to take for granted. These insights and the discovery of the real pleasure of working together on projects led us to the idea of doing *Twins on Twins.*

Glamour cover of the Gates twins, 1965. Photographed by Frances.

After photographic sessions with the Kienast quints.
Kathryn carries Ted back home.

Frances photographing Vivian and Marian Brown
in San Francisco for *Twins on Twins*.

Left to right: the Clendenin, Savage
and Woodie twins.

The Hattery twins.
Karla and Kevin, Karen and Kent, two sets of twins in
one family, the children of Max and Sue Hattery.

INTERNATIONAL TWINS ASSOCIATION

Each year, nearly one thousand twins gather for the convention of the International Twins Association. Some of the twins have never missed an annual meeting since the ITA began forty-five years ago. The ITA requires two things of its members: that each was born a twin and that each pay a $10 annual dues fee. Triplets, quadruplets and quintuplets are invited to join and a twin whose twin is deceased is welcomed by the group.

These photographs were taken at the 1979 ITA convention in Memphis, Tennessee. Dressing alike is part of the scene and the meetings are dominated by look-alike, dress-alike twins. Often the matching clothes are carefully put away until the next year's convention. The Twin Contest is the grand finale each year with twins competing in twenty-eight categories. The contest starts with a prize for the "Most Alike Infants in Arms" and proceeds with awards to the "Most Alike Men" and the "Most Alike Ladies" in nine age categories; then onto "The Twins Who Travel from Farthest Away," etc.

Sightseeing, a costume party and seminars or lectures on twin matters are the highlights of the three-day event. ITA tells its members: "Casual dress is recommended for most all convention activities, although it is nice to dress up for the Sunday evening dinner dance." At the 1979 convention a bellboy was heard saying, "It wouldn't pay to get drunk around here—you'd go bats!"

Robert and Didier Weiss.

"We weren't even aware of the organization and we've been twins for years—I'm fascinated with twins myself."

Linda and Lois Mann.

"We're *always* together!

Alice and Clarice Rainer.

"We think it's God's greatest honor on
earth to be made an identical twin."

Nora and Zora Shearer.

"Do you think that's a good idea—
the dressing alike, or not?"

Ruth and Esther Thieleman.

"When your twin is happy, you're naturally happy
too. We believe we are an extension of each other."

It's like Noah's Ark. There's two of everybody here.

I have friends who tell me that ever so many people think of twins as one person.

We come to ITA to be with other twins, and to share their experiences.

We did a lot of double-dating. We dressed alike until she got married.

Wow, do you ever feel pressure when your twin's dating and you're not!

Let twins be themselves, don't force them into society's mold. Twins can be as alike as two peas in a pod and still be individuals because they each have their own thoughts and feelings.

It's not uncommon to hear the comment: What happens to one will always happen to the other. I don't believe this.

In Abilene, Texas, we had to dress alike. Our Daddy would not have it any other way. He wanted us to be boys; so he raised us as athletes, but we had to be always dressed exactly alike. Even after she got married, when she'd come home, he'd buy her new clothes so she'd have some like mine.

I married an identical twin, Wilfred McCammon, and my name was McCammon, so I just changed my name from Miss to Mrs. It was uncanny. Both grandfathers were named John and both lived in Conway Springs, Kansas. My grandfather was a farmer; his grandfather was an Orient Railroad man.

Left to right: Mary Butler and May Bowen, Juanita Bush and Janet Hickman, Evia Sage and Eva Jeter, Pauline and Paulette Fahnstock, Alice and Clarice Rainer. In front: Jennifer and Michelle King.

Some parents want to raise them both the same. Always look-alike, always dress-alike, always go to the same places. Now I think the trend is to wean the twins from each other. I don't think that's such a good idea; we always enjoyed being together.

Society compares us; the media compares us; but our parents never did. Here comparison is a dirty word!

We had to dress alike just because we were twins. When we had company they would always like to tell us apart. They would look us over real well and they'd see a little hole somewhere in a sock or something. They'd say, 'Uh-huh I'll be able to tell.' If we found out what it was, we'd go behind the piano and change stockings, and then they'd be fooled.

We want the organization to expand. We want to bring in others because we think there is a message here.

What really hurts in school more than the competition is the comparison. He was better in some subjects and I was better in others.

As children if one of us knew something, we thought the other one knew it too.

Left to right: Don and Dave Carroll, Dollie Maxwell and Ollie Adams, Anita Tracy with daughters, Michelle and Dannielle, Sindy and Sandy Blevins, Ervwin and Everett Courrier.

Group of 270 twins at the ITA Convention, Memphis, Tennessee. September 1979.

NOTES

1. Michael Grant, *Roman Myths* (New York: Charles Scribner's Sons, 1971), p. 189.
2. Gunnar Dahlberg, "An Explanation of Twins," *Scientific American* (January 1951), p. 48.
3. Edward Ziegler, "The Mysterious Bonds of Twins," *Reader's Digest* (January 1980), p. 79.
4. Ibid.
5. Stanley L. Weinberg, *Biology: An Inquiry Into the Study of Life* (Rockleigh, N.J.: Allyn & Bacon, Inc., 1974), p. 519.
6. "Brother's Keeper," *Look* (February 1979), pp. 82–83.
7. Lawrence K. Altman, *New York Times* (May 29, 1977), Section 4, p. 7.
8. Blair Rogers, M.D., "Genetics of Transplantation in Humans," *Diseases of the Nervous System*, vol. 24, no. 4 (April 1963).
9. Marilyn H. Houlberg, "Ibeji Images of the Yoruba," *African Arts*, vol. 7, no. 1 (Autumn 1973), p. 25.
10. George Devereux, "Mohave Beliefs Concerning Twins," *American Anthropologist*, N.S. 43 (1941), p. 574.
11. Ibid, p. 575.
12. Ibid.
13. Ibid, pp. 580–81.
14. Edwin M. Loeb, "The Twin Cult in the Old and New World," *International Congress of Americanists, Miscellanea Paul Rivet octogenario dicata* (Mexico: n.p., 1958), p. 152.
15. E. Sidney Hartland, "Twins," *Encyclopedia of Religion and Ethics* (Edinburgh and New York: Charles Scribner's Sons, 1958), vol. 12, p. 497.
16. I. Schapera, "Customs Relating to Twins in South Africa," *Journal of the African Society*, vol. 26, no. 12 (1927), p. 127.
17. Hartland, "Twins," p. 495.
18. Ibid, p. 491.
19. Laila Williamson, "Infanticide: An Anthropological Analysis," *Infanticide and the Value of Life* (New York: Prometheus Books, 1978), p. 72.
20. Rene Zazzo, "Genesis and Peculiarities of the Personality of Twins," *Twin Research: Psychology and Methodology* (New York: Alan R. Liss, Inc., 1978), pp. 1–11.
21. *Reader's Digest* (January 1980), pp. 81, 82.
22. Louis Keith and Michael John Hughey, "Twin Gestation," *Gynecology and Obstetrics* (Hagerstown, MD: Harper & Row, 1979), vol. 2, chapter 74, p. 1.
23. Rosemary T. Theroux, and Josephine F. Tingley, *The Care of Twin Children* (Chicago: Center for The Study of Multiple Gestation, 1978).

BIBLIOGRAPHY

Adams, Marie Jeanne. "Sacred Children in the Ritual and Art of the Yoruba of Nigeria." In *Symbols.* Boston: The Peabody Museum and Harvard University, Winter 1980.

Abbott, Lyman. *Silhouettes of My Contemporaries.* Garden City and Toronto: Doubleday, Page and Co., 1921.

Albert, Maurice. *La Culte de Castor et Pollux en Italie.* Paris: Bibliothèque des Ecoles Françaises d'Athenes et de Rome, 1883.

Alexander, Hartley B. *The Mythology of All Races.* Vol. 10. New York: Cooper Square Publishers, Inc., 1964.

Allen, Richard Hinckley. *Star Names: Their Lore and Meaning.* New York: Dover Publications, 1963.

Altman, Lawrence K. "Transplants: Shortage of Donors Is Still Acute." *New York Times*, May 29, 1977.

Andretti, Mario. *What's It Like Out There?* Chicago: H. Regnery Co., 1970.

Belo, Jane. "A Study of Customs Pertaining to Twins in

Bali." *Tijdschrift voor indische taaland en volkenkunde.* Vol. 75, 1935.

Bolton, Isabel. *Under Gemini.* New York: Harcourt, Brace and World, 1966.

Brinton, Daniel G. *The Myths of the New World: A Treatise on the Symbolism and Mythology of the Red Race of America.* Philadelphia: David McKay, 1896.

"Brother's Keeper." *Look,* February 1979, pp. 82–83.

Campbell, Joseph. *The Masks of God: Occidental Mythology.* Vol. 3, 4th ed. New York: Viking Press, 1972.

Chen, Edwin. "Twins Reared Apart: A Living Lab." *New York Times Magazine,* December 19, 1979.

Clymer, Floyd. *Steam Car Scrapbook.* New York: Bonanza Books, 1945.

Dahlberg, Gunnar. "An Explanation of Twins." *Scientific American,* January 1951.

Devereux, George. "Mohave Beliefs Concerning Twins." *American Anthropologist.* N.S. 43, 1941.

"Dioscuri." *Standard Dictionary of Folklore.* New York, 1949.

Dorman, S. S. "Some Beliefs and Ceremonies Connected with the Birth and Death of Twins Among the South African Natives." *South African Journal of Science.* Vol. 29, 1932.

Fröhner, W. *Deux Peintures de Vases Grecs de la Necropole de Kameiros.* Paris: J. Baur et Detaille, 1871.

Gardner, Percy. *Types of Greek Coins.* Cambridge: n.p., 1883.

Gedda, Luigi. *Twins in History and Science.* Springfield, Ill.: Charles C. Thomas, 1961.

Gleason's Pictorial Drawing Room Companion, March 19, 1853.

Goodrich, Lloyd. *Raphael Soyer.* New York: Whitney Museum of Art, 1967.

Grant, Michael. *Roman Myths.* New York: Charles Scribner's Sons, 1971.

Granzberg, Gary. "Twin Infanticide—A Cross-Cultural Test of a Materialistic Explanation." *Ethos.* Vol. 1, No. 4, 1973.

Hagedorn, Judy, and Janet Kizziar. *Gemini: The Psychology and Phenomena of Twins.* Anderson, S.C.: Droke House-Hallux, 1974.

Harris, J. Rendel. *The Cult of the Heavenly Twins.* Cambridge: The University Press, 1906.

———. *The Dioscuri in the Christian Legends.* London: n.p., 1903.

Hartland, E. Sidney. "Twins." *Encyclopedia of Religion and Ethics.* Vol. 12. Edinburgh and New York: Charles Scribner's Sons, 1958.

Houlberg, Marilyn H. "Ibeji Images of the Yoruba." *African Arts.* Vol. 7, 1973.

Hunt, Morton M. "Doctor Kallmann's 7000 Twins." *Saturday Evening Post,* November 6, 1954.

Jamison, Andrew. *The Steam-Powered Automobile.* Indiana: Indiana University Press, 1970.

Jeffreys, W., M.D. "The Cult of Twins Among Some African Tribes." *South African Journal of Science.* Vol. 58, 1963.

Kallman, Franz J. *Heredity in Mental Health and Disorders.* New York: W. W. Norton & Co., 1953.

Keith, Louis, M.D., and Michael John Hughey, M.D. "Twin Gestation." *Gynecology and Obstetrics.* Vol. 2, 1979.

Krappe, Alexandre Haggerty. *Mythologie Universelle.* Paris: Payot, 1930.

Lang, Andrew, ed. "The Boys with the Golden Stars." In *The Violet Fairy Book.* London: Longman, Green, and Co., 1901.

Levy, Jerrold E. "The Fate of Navajo Twins." *American Anthropologist.* Vol. 66, No. 4, 1964.

Livy. *Loeb Classical Library.* Cambridge: Harvard University Press, 1952.

Loeb, Edwin M. "The Twin Cult in the Old and New World." In *International Congress of Americanists, Miscellanea Paul Rivet octogenario dicata.* Mexico: n.p., 1958.

Metraux, A. "Twin Heroes in South American Mythology." *Journal of American Folklore.* Vol. 59, 1946.

Newhall, Beaumont. *The History of Photography.* New York: Museum of Modern Art and George Eastman House, 1964.

Newman, Horatio. *Multiple Human Births: Twins, Triplets, Quadruplets, and Quintuplets.* New York: Doubleday, Doran & Co., 1940.

———. *The Physiology of Twinning.* Chicago: University of Chicago Press, 1922.

Picart Le Romain, B. *The Temple of the Muses.* Amsterdam: Chatelain, 1733.

Piwonka, Ruth, and Roderic H. Blackburn. *Ammi Phillips in Columbia County: A Catalogue of an Exhibition of Portraits Done in Columbia County by Ammi Phillips (1788–1865).* Kinderhook, N.Y.: 1975.

———. *A Visible Heritage: A History in Art and Architecture.* Kinderhook, N.Y.: Columbia County Historical Society, 1977.

Rogers, Blair O., M.D. "Genetics of Transplantation in Humans." *Diseases of the Nervous System,* Monograph Supplement. Vol. 24, No. 4, 1963.

Runk, Emma. *The Ten Broeck Family Genealogy.* New York: De Vinne Press, 1897.

Schapera, I. "Customs Relating to Twins in South Africa." *Journal of the African Society.* Vol. 26, No. 12, 1927.

Sirota, Len. "Twins of Yorubaland." *Bulletin of Field Museum of Natural History.* Vol. 38, No. 7, 1967.

Smith, Richard D. "How the Other Half Lives: Twins and Science." *The Sciences,* February 1979.

Soyer, Raphael. *Diary of an Artist.* Washington, D.C.: New Republic Books, 1977.

Stevenson, Isobel. "Twins as Magicians and Healing Gods." *Ciba Symposium.* Vol. 2, No. 10, 1941.

Letters of Harriet Beecher Stowe. Cambridge, Mass.: Stowe-Day Library Collection, Schlesinger Library, Radcliffe College.

Theroux, Rosemary T., and Josephine F. Tingley. *The Care of Twin Children.* Chicago: The Center for Study of Multiple Gestation, 1978.

Thompson, Robert. *Black Gods and Kings,* "Chapter 13." Bloomington, Ind.: Indiana University Press, 1975.

Thwaites, Ruben Gold, ed. *Jesuit Relations and Allied Documents.* Vol. 10, No. 24. Cleveland: The Burrows Brothers, 1896.

"The Twin Sisters." In *The Photographic World.* Vol. 2, 1872.

Weinberg, Stanley L. *Biology: An Inquiry into the Study of Life.* Rockleigh, N.J.: Allyn and Bacon, Inc., 1974.

Willard, Charlotte. *Moses Soyer.* Cleveland and New

York: World Publishing Company, 1967.

Williamson, Laila. "Infanticide: An Anthropological Analysis." *Infanticide and the Value of Life.* New York: Prometheus Books, 1978.

Zazzo, Rene. "Genesis and Peculiarities of the Personality of Twins." In *Progress in Clinical and Biological Research.* Vol. 24, Part A. New York: Alan R. Liss, 1978.

Ziegler, Edward. "The Mysterious Bond of Twins." *Reader's Digest,* January 1980.

NATIONAL TWIN ORGANIZATIONS

International Twins Association
Elspeth (Beth) Corley and Beverley (Bebe) Simmons
P.O. Box #77386, Station C
Atlanta, Georgia, 30357

National Organization of Mothers of Twins Clubs, Inc.
Executive Office
5402 Amberwood Lane
Rockville, Maryland 20853
Telephone: (301) 460-9108

The Center for Study of Multiple Gestation
Suite 463-5
333 East Superior Street
Chicago, Illinois 60611
Telephone: (312) 266-9093

INDEX

Page entries in boldface refer to illustrations.

THE AUTHORS

KATHRYN MCLAUGHLIN ABBE and FRANCES McLAUGHLIN GILL are photographers whose work has been acclaimed both here and abroad. Both are graduates of Pratt Institute; both have had their photographs exhibited in many museums and galleries, including the Metropolitan Museum of Art and the Brooklyn Museum. Their work is familiar to readers of publications such as *Glamour, Good Housekeeping, Parents' Magazine, McCall's,* and *Vogue.* Kathryn is the coauthor of *Stars of the Twenties,* a book of photographs. Frances's credits include *Face Talk, Hand Talk, Body Talk,* a graphic book for children, and *Spiral from the Sea: An Anthropological Look at Shells* written by Jane Safer, published by Clarkson N. Potter.

Kathryn lives with her husband, James Abbe, on Long Island, and they are parents of two sons and a daughter. Frances and her daughter, an architect, live in New York City.

A NOTE ON THE TYPE

The text of this book was set in Palatino, designed in 1948 by the German typographer Hermann Zapf and issued between 1950 and 1952. Palatino is distinguished by its broad letters and vigorous, inclined serifs. Named after Giovanbattista Palatino, it was the first Zapf typeface to be introduced to America.

The display type is a modern redesigned version of a Caslon specimen of 1734. William Caslon, born in 1692 at Cradley in Worcestershire, turned to letter founding after being apprenticed to an engraver of ornamental gunlocks and barrels. There was nothing startlingly new about his designs; he took as his models the best Dutch types of the seventeenth century, particularly those of Van Dijck. The fact that he started an era of great British typography was due less to his originality than to his competence and ability at engraving and casting types at a time when letter founding in England was at a very low ebb.

The book was composed by Adroit Graphic Composition Inc., in New York City and printed in offset on seventy pound Mead Matte by Halliday Lithograph in West Hanover, Massachusetts. It was bound by The Book Press in Brattleboro, Vermont.

Edited by Carol Southern
Production supervision by Teresa Nicholas
Designed by Hermann Strohbach